The

Enchanted

Forest

POCKET EDITION

Published from
The Joshua Free Imprint – JFI Publications
Mardukite Borsippa HQ, San Luis Valley, Colorado
Founding Church of Mardukite Zuism,
Mardukite Academy & Systemology Society
for religious and educational purposes only.

The

enchanted

forest

A DRUID'S GRIMOIRE OF CELTIC TREE MAGIC

Based on the work by Joshua Free
Edited by Rowen Gardner

THE JOSHUA FREE IMPRINT
JFI PUBLICATIONS

© 2023, JOSHUA FREE

ISBN : 979-8-9871249-7-0

Premiere Pocket Paperback Edition — *April 2023*

Mardukite Druidism (Grade-I, D-Series)

mardukite.com

Veiled Secrets of the Forest are Revealed!

Awaken the forest to your presence, learn to communicate with trees, discover how they communicate with each other, fashion a staff and collection of wands, and perform rituals fulfilling your role as Guardian of the Grove.

Open the door to the ancient forest mysteries! Now you can easily explore and understand the physical and magical properties of sacred forest trees and their enchanted wood. Discover what lessons hide behind the foliage once only known to the Druids of old.

Beginners and adepts alike will find that "The Enchanted Forest" is a handbook worth its weight in gold!

Joshua Free has been paving the way through these woodland facets of nature magick for over 25 years, and now presents this revised portion of the "Elvenomicon" volume as a stand-alone pocket guide for the first time!

"The Enchanted Forest" is your key to unlock the powerful system of forest magick preserved in the Celtic-Druid and Elven-Faerie traditions.

If you want the best guide possible as your companion on your magical woodland journey, then "The Enchanted Forest" by Joshua Free is the ideal practical manual for you to access the ancient druidcraft of Celtic Tree Magick.

Titles in the forthcoming
2023 pocket paperback series
based on the "*Elvenomicon*"
by Joshua Free

Complete series coming soon
from JFI Publications

Elvenomicon Series-I

The Secret Book of Elven-Faerie

The Elven-Faerie Grimoire

The Enchanted Forest

Elvenomicon Series-II

Secret Legacy of Elves & Faeries

The Elven-Faerie Spellbook

The Book of Ogham

TABLET OF CONTENTS

INTRODUCTION

by Joshua Free

My participation in the legacy behind "*The Enchanted Forest*" began in the mid-1990's during a critical resurgence of 'New Age' revival—and foremost among the interests: the *Celts* and *Druids*.

The Enchanted Forest is an integral part of a greater body of work pertaining to my own personal involvement with *Elven-Faerie* traditions of Druidism for over 25 years. This material was imparted to me directly by a first-hand personal 'apprenticeship' with its modern developers and is reflected in what I presented as the <u>Elvenomicon</u> series.

The original "*Elvenomicon*" series—a trilogy in one volume—first circulated in the underground as "*The Book of Elven-Faerie*," but I later renamed as *Elvenomicon* to avoid confusing the total collection of work with the title of the first discourse it contained: *Book of Elven-Faerie*—retitled *Secret Book of Elven-Faerie* for this present series reissue. It is a separate volume from the other two parts in the trilogy: *The Elven-Faerie Grimoire* and

Greenwood Forest Grimoire—the later being presented as this present tome: "*The Enchanted Forest.*" But, collectively, this trilogy comprises the *Elvenomicon* 'Series-1' and the contents of my own original presentation of Elven-Faerie Druidry for the past 20 years.

'Celtic Tree Mysteries' occupy intellectual and spiritual attention of all serious Druids or practitioners of the Elven-Faerie magical traditions. As one who continues to be enamored by the enchanting relationship that is maintained between Druid and 'Nature', the work toward codifying and systematizing Oghamic lore has been ongoing now for over a quarter-of-a-century, never seeming complete enough for a release into 'static' book form. It represents 'living knowledge' of the Earth that is constantly evolving. As such, although mentioned in no less than six of my previous publications, I have not presented a definitive *Book of Ogham* before, but such may now be found as a 'Series-2' companion to this present volume.

The Book of Ogham picks up where *Greenwood Forest Grimoire* ('*The Enchanted Forest*') leaves off in the first *Elvenomicon* series/anthology.

And it is the *Greenwood Forest Grimoire*—or *'Enchanted Forest'*—material that will occupy our attentions presently.

Many have asked me why 'such-and-such' wasn't included as tree correspondences for *'Enchanted Forest'*. My answer remains that the first *Elvenomicon* series did not so much reflect my personal opinion or modern research as it did the preservation of a very specific 'Elven-Faerie' Druidic tradition and the lore representing it. Therefore, I did not unnecessarily alter what I was given. I had to focus my attention on writing the bulk of the background and introductions for each section in order to prepare a 'book version' of a hand-written work I had copied down from an underground tradition. The actual rites and correspondences, I left alone.

It may also be noted that *Greenwood Forest Grimoire* (*'The Enchanted Forest'*)—of the first *Elvenomicon* series—focuses on 'trees' themselves; not necessarily Ogham. *'Enchanted Forest'* emphasizes physical tree properties and related 'magical' lore, whereas *'Book of Ogham'*, in Series-2, examines more oracular lore (divination) in Oghamic tradition.

It becomes apparent to a seasoned, well-acquainted, Seeker, that *Elvenomicon* Series-2 bridges the 'Elven-Faerie' tradition with my 'Pheryllt Researches' in combination with other critical 'New Age' systems that have come (and often gone) during the past few decades leaving their footprints behind, reminding us of their own ventures to uncover secrets of the Great Mystery Tradition.

Many key contributions to the foundation of the *Elvenomicon* began in the 1970's and were revised in the late-1980's prior to a 'New Age' revival of interest in the Ogham as a divinatory system—something which seems to have emerged directly following a release of '*The Celtic Tree Oracle*' by Liz and Colin Murray in 1988. This contributed to later revisions of this work once it passed into my hands in the 1990's. Most of my additions have been reserved for a companion '*Book of Ogham*' volume. *The Enchanted Forest* offers Seekers the most practical and concise guide to 'forest magick' and 'Celtic Tree Mysteries'. Enjoy the journey!

—Joshua Free, Spring Equinox 2023
Borsippa HQ, San Luis Valley

THE
GREENWOOD
FOREST
GRIMOIRE

the magick of the enchanted forest

Green is the universal color of Life and Nature—a color most sacred in Elven-Faerie Tradition, from which the *"Green World"* is named: the "place of enchantment" where "Forest Magick" permeates the air. True "Elven Magick" is performed in the "Green World" and pertains to its elements more strongly than any other magical system. The place of operation for this "Green Magic" is *in* Nature itself—no dank chambers or elaborate ceremonial vaults will do. The *"Green World"* is described in lore as that space in the physical world that resonates an affinity with all natural energies of the Elemental Kingdoms—and therefore raw forces of Cosmic energy may be tapped, unhindered by the intrusion and tampering of humans. Practice of "Forest Magick," by definition, is primarily concerned with the Earth and Air Elements. It is in these forms and manifestations that an Elven Wizard, Mystic or Druid is able to use to capture the essence of "Earth Magic" as related to trees.

In Elven-Faerie Druidry, a "*silva*" (or '*sylva*') is a magical treatise or discourse cataloging the nature and function of the forests—with psychological, spiritual and emotion properties coinciding with physical lore. Most current forms of "tree magic" linked to the Druid "*Ogham*" (also spelled "*Ogam*") are derived from the "*Book of Ballymote*"—also known as the "*Sylva d'Ogam*." That information is collected in a separate volume in this series titled: "*The Book of Ogham*."

Our present volume examines the "Greenwood Grimoire" from the original *Elvenomicon* series. It is based on—and includes—a manual titled '*Sylva Druieachd*' which means "Treatise of Forest Wizards" or "Treatise on Elven Forest Magick" within the same tradition that provided the present author with materials for the "*Elven-Faerie Grimoire*." For those with a deep inclination toward "Tree Magic," this book will serve as an incredibly faithful guide to the Enchanted Forest.

It is important, from the start, to address an idea put forth by anthropologists called "tree worship." Ancient Druids, Elves, Mystics and Wizards *did not* "worship" trees any more than a person might worship some other sacred symbol used to represent the "Divine" in a religion. Elves *revere* trees as an icon of the ALL, the Source-of-all-Being and the Cosmic Law that guides and defines all existence. By understanding the trees and the way in which they grow, Elves also understood the expansiveness of fractal existence of Reality long before and far clearer than Fibonacci and other modern mathematicians.

All life, matter and energy across space and time is a progression of Cosmic Law that moves or grows in the same manner, code or program as trees. This is an important key to the system of Elven Magick. It is often thought that trees are simply inanimate and unintelligent beings, and yet this could not be more untrue. Although they may not share the same degree of "movement freedom" as many other creatures in the wild, their "Earth memory" is far older, clearer and more accessible than what is encoded in shorter-lived beings.

Trees also have an ability to be charged (absorb energy) from their natural surroundings, and like other lifeforms, prefer to live in "groups" and "communities." They also like to communicate with one another.

"Awakened" trees—those interacting with active Elven magick—will more easily communicate with one another, and if there is a shortage of trees to talk to, they will produce them, through "*layrs.*" The branches or roots will actually re-root to form a new tree, while still connected to the mother. The more we interact with them and learn, the more we realize that trees are actually quite sentient beings. They have the ability to communicate with us when their spirit is "Awakened" or "remembered" intentionally with Elven high magick.

Traditional lore describes the "spirit of a tree" as a "*Dryad*"—borrowing the Greek term used to define a female Druidess, or 'Lady of the Woods'. The *Dryad* "spirit" is an intelligence or spiritual growth program inhabiting and driving the living system manifestation that we call "*tree.*"

The same patterns of tree-like consciousness are seen in neural formations of the brain called "*dendrytes*"—the word "*Dryte*" is a masculine equivalent to "*Dryad*."

The "spirits" within the trees—which have many names in the Elven Tradition—are a part of any wood taken from it for magical purposes, just as a fractal or genetic print retains the entire code within each part. In fact, nearly all tools used in Elven Forest Magick are crafted from trees. It is the manner in which the wood is taken and how it is used that distinguishes the Elven Way from the ways of Humans. This begins with a high reverence for the Green World and all life in Nature, including asking permission from the spirits of a tree before taking any part of its lifeforce. We see a similar practice among both archaic shamans and modern herbalists. By "permission seeking," a practitioner further develops a communicable relationship with the Green World—and this is reinforced in consciousness with each "communion."

With exception of the title for this "grimoire," the term 'wood' is hereafter applied to parts of a tree no longer attached to a living tree—either from intentional removal, or some other natural means. There are essentially three types of "*wood*" indexed by loremasters of Elven-Faerie Druid Tradition:—

> *Deadwood / Dredgewood*
> *Wickwood / Wetwood**
> *Livewood / Wizardwood*

Wood that you find littered all throughout the forest floor is *deadwood*. For whatever reason, it has been broken away from the trees—and it naturally does—mixing with fallen leaves and decaying foliage to form soil after its decomposition. It is good for kindling fire, but be sure not to completely clear it away from the forest floor, as it is a necessary part of the ecosystem. Deadwood may be used for amulets, talismans and various magical crafts, but is not traditionally preferred for permanent ritual tools. A wizard may enjoy the discovery of a perfect wood specimen for a wand or staff already broken away from a tree. There are no absolute rules that discourage this; only many suggestions regarding cutting live trees.

---

* Called "*greenwood*" in some former versions.

Wickwood is *any* wood taken from the living forest that is not properly removed by a magical practitioner. This means any wood harvested as lumber or broken by carelessness without following Elven-Faerie codes of permission. When wood is taken in this manner, the spirits of the tree actually retract from it, making it quite unsuitable for magical work, particularly of the Elven-Druid variety. Humans have a tendency to remove plants and trees with hostility and ignorance. Such energy is also present in wood harvested by that same sentiment.

Wizardwood is that wood taken from a living tree by an Elven Wizard, Druid or Herbalist following Elven-Faerie codes. This includes permission and thanks for its sacrifice. The article removed will respectfully preserve the spiritual essence of the living spirit of the tree—as a result the wood is blessed by "Nature spirits" and is positively charged with perfect love, peace and cosmic unity. If you feel inclined to leave an offering to these "Nature spirits" in exchange for their sacrifice, then by all means do so. *Always follow your intuition when walking the path through the enchanted forest!*

elven high magick

Many techniques of Elven High Magick are categorized as "energy work," "light work," or "astral work" using New Age vocabulary. An ability to use currents of natural or cosmic energy in "magick" is dependent on the true understanding and realization of a "higher omni-dimensional web-matrix" or "field" in which all energy exists and acts beyond the surface images and forms we believe we are interacting with. It is really this underlying energy that is exchanging and moving, and only bands of light within a specific spectrum give rise to visible manifestations in the "world we see."

It is essential that an Elven Wizard is fluent in their knowledge and use of the "subtle" underlying currents of universal cosmic energy found throughout all Nature and within and as all Life. These frequencies or vibrations—often interpreted as "auric energy"—emanate from all systems: people; animals; trees; rocks; minerals ...*everything*. Certain individuals may even increase their sensitivity to regularly perceive these energetic interactions at the most basic underlying degrees of awareness. A kaleidoscope of energetic currents or "rays" are abundantly processing around you—and through you. Energies transmitted through all environments, actions and thoughts are in constant interaction with each another, even when we are not "aware" or do not see a visible change.

Try this exercise:—Go outside on a clear day when the sky is light blue and lay down in the grass, perhaps on a hill. Allow your attention to drift as you quiet your mind. Focus on clouds, if any, or the blueness of the sky. Bring your awareness away from the things of a "mortal" world and life.

Raise your arm and hold your hand about a foot in front of your face so that your vision of the blue sky is backing it. Place your index finger and thumb together as if you are pinching something and rub the slowly in a circular swirling motion. Bring them apart about an inch and soften your gaze to look between them. *What do you see? What is that?*

Energy streams and strings are indeed all around us. They project from all living things and may be altered with emotion and intention. Even physical placement of non-living objects—as made famous in recent revivals of *"feng shui"*—has the the ability to affect the motion of energy currents around us, and in turn, our own vibrational states in their presence.

"Dowsing-With-Your-Feet" is a technique taught to Elven/Sylvan (Forest) Wizards that assists sensitivity development. They learn to free their minds and allow inner intuition to guide their "actions" when selecting a particular tree, rock, stick, *&tc*, which we might relay as having a particular aspect "speak to us," or that a particular tree *&tc* has "chosen" us. The relationship between a Wizard and the Green World is unique for each instance—and nearly impossible to "grade" as many have attempted in their formation of certain 'Orders' and 'Lodges'—which is why "Inner Teachings" are always revealed by Nature *herself*.

The core material in the *Elvenomicon* series is meant to provide an intrepid Seeker the keys necessary to unlock the "Great Mysteries" by sheer dedication and sincere desire. Potential "Forest Wizards" will have to enter the Green World for an extended period of time to work with these energies directly—yet, once we shared communion with these forces, the "Astral Grove" always exists within us to work from.

According to Elven Tradition, *all* trees have healing qualities. Almost any species of tree is capable of channeling pain and negative energies down into the magma core of the Earth for transformation. It may seem odd to send such energies down to the Earth to be incinerated, but they are more destructive when left unchecked on the surface.

Wizards must cure their own pain to properly ease the pain of anyone else—including the Earth itself. Equally so, it is actually in our best interests to help in relieving the suffering of the surface world—ourselves and our environment—so that it does not restrict the future global process of Ascension that we are all participating in.

In some ways, everything is connected together in the Universe—meaning all of *us*—and what one or two people may feel in one place, is not at all restricted to affecting only them alone. Every course we take sets out causal ripples or tides of manifestation across seas of infinity—and we must take the responsibility for every single one of them if we are to assume any "control" over their "power."

You might practice "Dowsing-With-Your-Feet" for intuitively selecting a "Healing Tree" to perform the following exercise. Ask the tree's permission to heal your pain —emotional, physical, &tc.—then soften your gaze and attempt to perceive a visible auric glow emanating from the tree, similar to the bands you may have seen between your fingers in a previous exercise. Sit up straight with your back to the tree—using its trunk to support your spine, keeping sure you are in a comfortable position. Feel and see your "auric body" merge with that of the tree.

Focus on your connection to the tree until you no longer easily distinguish boundaries between your body and the tree. Bring your pains to the surface and send them down the trunk into the ground with each breath.

Feel and see that you and the tree are pushing it deep down into the fiery core below for incineration and recycling. You may wish to visualize any remaining energetic cords or ties to the energy as equally dissolved. Always thank the Nature-spirits when you have completed energy work in the "Green World." It is also customary to "tend to"—or "groom," in the Animal Kingdom—the fellow life in Nature that we are stewards of or share kinship with, furthering our ecological responsibility.

Whenever activating your consciousness within and as an "astral form"—just as you would in order to partake in 'astral travel'— you enter your "Light Body" or *a* "Body of Light." If you do this in wakened states without the intention of Astral Projection, you may be able to use this shift in consciousness as a catalyst for better recognizing 'subtle energies', 'streams' and 'strings' that seem otherwise invisible to the uninitiated. This "astral preparation" technique is the same method used for other 'energy work', 'light work' and Tree Magick.

Entering the "Light Body" is an application of Visualization and Will to direct intention —just as in all other 'energy play' and 'light work'. Such methods differ greatly from the vocal dramas and ceremonial forms of ritual magic popular in other systems, including "Elementalism." Energy currents of the forest are strong, but are slow in their build-up of "eventual power."

"Forest Magick" does not carry the same 'flare of immediate accessibility' that many practitioners search for—such as we see in the more active Elements of Nature and its corresponding "spirit world." In the forests, progressive learning and communication efforts tend to be slower—matching speeds of frequency in the Green World. To participate in "woodland magic," a Sylvan Wizard slows their vibrations to the "heartbeat of the forest" and envision their own "light-shield" as the same brilliant emerald green.

Try this:—Sit comfortably with your back erect or lie down. I do not suggest sitting cross-legged, with any parts of the body crossing, or without back support, when first attempting. Begin by focusing all your awareness as a light in your feet, initially drawing this energy up from the ground, and concentrate all your focus and awareness on this area until it is completely filled with light. Slowly bring this light awareness throughout your entire body, moving it from your toes, feet, ankles, legs and knees upward into your thighs, pelvic region, solar plexus, stomach, chest and shoulders, then finally into your arms, neck, head and reaching its destination in forming a halo-crown about the top of your head. By this method, the Wizard becomes a "Pillar of Light." Feel this light extending from your body and strengthening your auric shield. [The "Western magical tradition" even observes a similar version of this rite, called the "Middle Pillar."]

Accessing the "Astral World" begins first with the ability to project one's consciousness into their "Light Body." Secondly, the Wizard consciously detaches their "Light Body" from its fixed awareness to the physical simulacrum that it localizes as a "home" or "genetic vehicle" (for the physical degree of material existence within the Human range of normative sensory perception). In Forest Magick, the Wizard does not detach into the astral, but maintains this heightened sense of awareness as a magical prerequisite to performing any light-work or energy-work—in Nature or otherwise. The Shaman that visits the "Otherworld" to perform their "magic" does this too. Rather than performing a ritual or ceremony within the physical *Nemeton*, the magic is conducted directly on the "Astral Plane" within the "Astral Grove" or some other locale.

"Astral Travel" taps an imaginative part of our consciousness that is most active in children before civic systemology takes a greater hold on neural activity. But we are all "Children of Light" and "Children of the Stars"—and it is that "star-light" for which the "*astral*" is named. By raising our consciousness and awareness to connect with that ancient source of our *Self*, we are reaching closest to the light to become the free spirits again that we once knew as children, to partake in the amazing spiritual bliss that results from communion with the ALL. To visit your "Astral Grove" it is critical that you first become proficient in entering your "Light Body."

Once you're able to enter the "Light Body," practice of "Astral Travel" may be achieved by envisioning a catalyst for teleportation— meaning a 'threshold,' 'gateway' or 'portal,' to launch your astral form through. The Water element is a powerful "portal" ele- ment—representing the most fluid-like, yet physical, essence that bridges between "worlds." Females will find a sense of fa- miliarity using dark pools and mirrors as a doorway. The "Earth portal" or stone mega- lithic "Trilithon" gateway is another stereo- typical "portal" icon, popularly used in Druidism. Other Personal symbols or glyphs may be used to direct awareness as you pass into "Faerie."

Whatever method you choose, you project your conscious awareness into your Light Body and then project that body through an envisioned portal or representation of a door. This helps trigger the subconscious into releasing Awareness (or the mind) into the "Astral Field" and appropriates our at- tention awareness in the process. Simply envision the portal firmly, seeing it stand- ing before you in your mind's eye. Some practitioners have also found success by visualizing a "Flaming Door." Spend time practicing and refining your skills in assuming this state. Note all of its details of the visualization until it seems as real as any other experience. Using Will, you may direct your astral form through the portal, and maintain a belief that you occupy *this* physical body in the "Astral."

Once you have successfully launched yourself through the imagined portal, anything might occur. You may emerge in darkness—the Underworld Initiation—in which you will be forced to move your mind through a complex labyrinth, often a result of blocks or barriers of the uninitiated mind. You may find yourself in a "astral stellar void"—where all kinds and natures of energy and light moves this way and that, existing as "waves of possibility" and never really taking on a concrete form in one shape or another, known as the "White Place." Or, perhaps you will cross to the Abyss and find the shell of the void—before the First Cause—where all is the Infinity of Nothingness.

If you fix in your mind the intention to reach the "Astral Grove" upon entering this state of consciousness, then you may arrive in a 'greenwood forest setting'.

The "Astral Grove" is within the "*Infinite Enchanted Forest,*" and if you do not directly arrive there from your portal, you must "will" yourself there. Your "Astral Grove" is composed of infinite streams of light and energy, formed and constructed by your intentions. Nothing on the astral plane has form except as a finite perspective of an individual observer experiences it and interacts with it. Thus, there is a lot of room for games, magical practice and other experience in the Otherworld, especially if your access to a physical grove is limited.

the enchanted trees, forests and groves

"Elemental Magick" is explored within the *'Elven-Faerie Grimoire'* volume of this series. It is usually practiced within a ritually consecrated 'circle'. "Forest Magick" of Elven-Ffayrie Druidic tradition also uses a circle: a natural clearing for rites, one that is in the midst of a "grove" of trees. This "grove" is treated as the *Nemeton* for an Elven Wizard.

"Groves" were once intentionally planted and tended by Elvish Drwyds or Druids. A ring of specific species of tree and plantlife was maintained as an observatory-temple. The concept of a "tree calendar" most likely emerged from such practices, where wise Wizards were capable of literally "reading the signs of Nature" and interpreting natural conditions from the appearance of these trees—including the time of season.

Many have assumed that Ogham lore is primarily a means of "fortune-telling" or mundane divination, yet these natural observations could also predict weather, aniimal behaviors and other natural effects of the environment. Certain times of year, or other natural conditions, were reflected by the different species of the grove in specific ways—and this lore was carefully observed and cryptically recorded.

Elven Forest Magick lore describes no requirements concerning the boundary of a "ritual circle" or its marking. Large stones are not always appropriate, and they may even disrupt natural energies of groves and clearings that may already visibly appear as distinct "circles." Practice of Forest Magick is less formal, and more intentionally deliberate, than "ritual magic"—even when performed in a woodland setting. A practitioner might carry a small pouch of smaller gems/stones used to temporarily designate points of the circle or as a focal aid.

Circle stations are not often clearly indicated in the rites of Forest Magick as they are in Elementalism and traditional ritual magic—unless they are intended for groups. This is because magical work performed by Forest Wizards is primarily internal and often practiced alone. An urban citizen may find difficulties in planting and tending a physical grove. The ability to do this not only distinguishes the type of "magick" involved, but also the type of individual that is able to advance through the Elven Forest Magick system. The natural area guarded is revisited frequently for both mystical operations and meditative exercises which contribute a "charge" or quality of "Enchantment" to the terrain. The following groupings of tree species repeatedly appear in Elven-Faerie and Celtic-Druid lore:—

· The Elven-Ffayrie Triad Trees are *Oak, Ash* and *Thorn*.

· The Seven Chieftain Trees of the Cad Goddeu are *Apple, Ash, Hazel, Holly, Oak, Pine* and *Yew*.

· The Seven Noble Trees of the Grove are *Apple, Alder, Birch, Hazel, Holly, Oak* and *Willow*.

· The Nine Sacred Woods of Needfire include *Ash, Apple, Cedar, Hazel, Holly, Mistletoe, Oak, Pine* and *Poplar*.

· The Traditional Tree Calendar Grove consists of *Birch, Rowan, Alder, Willow,*

*Ash, Hawthorn, Oak, Holly, Hazel, Apple
(or Vine), Ivy, Reed (or Pine) and Elder.*

The "Greenwood Forest Grimoire" includes
several rites that may be used individually
or in succession as the application requires.

THE BLESSING OF THE SAPLINGS

Before planting a grove or breaking ground,
take all of the trees you intend to plant to
the location. All members of the "fellow-
ship" may also be present. Any participants
involved should perform all tree-work from
the "Body of Light." The leader (or land
steward) stands in the center and says:

> *Here I [we] have [are] gathered in this
> place of light. Here I [we] find a place to
> weave a Sacred Space that I wish to honor
> with the planting and stewardship of a
> Sacred Grove of trees. May this Holy Ne-
> meton be a place of peace and power.*

Conjure the circle, using stakes to mark its
boundary—marking where trees are to be
planted. Use the most appropriate liturgy.
Nature-spirits of the forest will not be as
concerned about your "ritual formalities"

as they will be with your planting.

NORTH: *I [we] come forth to this sacred place and call the spirits of the land to join us here. At this Nemeton do I [we] ask permissions to raise and tend a Sacred Grove of trees, following the tradition of my ancestors.*

EAST: *Here at this sacred place do I [we] acknowledge my [our] vow[s] as Keeper[s] of the Earth. Here I [we] pledge to be Guardian of the Grove, a consecrated Nemeton ever sacred. Here may the sylphs, sylves and Nature-spirits of the woodlands, come and bless, making holy and enchanted.*

SOUTH: *May these future trees of this Grove, these saplings presented here, be blessed by the good Creatures of Faerie, the Four Elements and the Sun above. May the light, love and strength of the cosmos nourish these trees and offer all life sanctuary when visiting here in peace and love.*

WEST—holding hands over buckets of water: *May the spirits and powers resid-*

ing in the Elements of Water, Sea and
Rain come forth and bless these vessels of
water. I use them to now share you bless-
ing with these saplings, that they may re-
ceive your grace. I ask that you be gener-
ous in nurturing this Sacred Grove with
your gentle life-giving rains.

Burn incense, carrying it thrice around the
circle boundary, clockwise. Feel the energy
in the area equalizing to the land changes
about to occur. Conjure a clear image of the
completed project and project it as you in-
form the spirits of Nature—and the trees to
be planted—of your intentions. Say:

By the grace and permission of the Forces
of Nature and the Spirits of the Universe;
in accordance with the covenant sworn
between my ancestors and the Ancient
and Shinning Ones; I now break ground in
perfect peace, perfect love and compas-
sion and understanding. I open this circle
now to perform the work, but the circle is
never broken.

CONSECRATION RITE FOR
A NEWLY PLANTED GROVE

After planting the grove trees, bring some remaining soil to the center of the grove circle and say:

> *May all good Spirits of the Earth and Land bless this soil, the land where it is used and the life in nourishes. Bless those who use it as an expression of perfect love to nurture this newly planted life.*

Bring this consecrated soil to each of the trees, sprinkling it over the topsoil around each one. Depending on species and climate, wood chips may be used if more appropriate. Feel the love and compassion for Nature and life flowing through you as you complete the planting stage for each of the trees. Return to the center to consecrate more water, saying:

> *May the Spirits of Water and Sea bless this water, the land where it is used and the life it nourishes. Bless those who use it in their expression of perfect love to nurture this newly planted life.*

Take the water around to each (as previously with soil). Then clean and clear the area before performing a "*Dedication.*"

THE RITE FOR PLANTING A SINGLE GUARDIAN TREE

This rite may be used to plant a specific "Guardian Tree" or it may be used for each tree planted in the "grove." Go to the space and ask the spirits of the land for permission before you break ground. Follow the basic steps outlined in previous rites—performing all work from a "Light Body." As you dig and plant the single tree, say:

> *I plant this tree in perfect peace, love, compassion and understanding. May it be to others and myself a symbol of the same.*

When are ready to complete the work with topsoil and/or woodchips, consecrate the materials, saying:

> *May this earth feed and nourish this sacred life, a symbol of perfect peace, love and compassion and understanding.*

Complete the planting, then consecrate vessels of water, saying:

> May this consecrated water bless and
> nourish the life of this sacred tree. May all
> good Elemental Spirits of Sea and Water
> ensure the rains to ever maintain it.

Water the tree liberally with your consecrated water and then connect with the aur-
ic/light field of the tree—something that
becomes easier as your proficiency in Tree
Magick grows—saying:

> By the Elements of Nature were you
> sown. By perfect peace and love are you
> grown. I am a Keeper of the Earth and
> have overseen your birth. I am a Guardi-
> an [Scion] of Elven Ways and your stew-
> ard for all my days.

Close the rite (if planting a single tree)—or
continue with each tree of the grove before
performing a "*Grove Dedication.*"

GROVE DEDICATION & STEWARDSHIP

A grove is consecrated and dedicated prior
to its use as a *Nemeton*. The rite may also be
used repeatedly over time. You may even

use this rite to dedicate existing groves growing in the wild.

NORTH: *May the Sacred Grove awaken to the mysteries of the Everlasting Forest. May it grant Elven Wizards, and those who come in peace, the same strength and protection the Sacred Grove offered the Ancients. May the sacred ground on which it stands, be purified and blessed.*

EAST: *Here now before the Sacred Grove and the Nature-spirits awakened and drawn to my work, do I vow stewardship to the Sacred Grove and the mysteries of the Everlasting Forest. I am a Guardian of the Earth Mother, keeper and protector of her ancient ways.*

SOUTH: *I summon forth the energy and power of the Sky and Sun. Come forth spirit that grants light and life to all creatures on the Earth. Send forth thy Rays of Radiance and instill strength and well-being throughout the Sacred Grove.*

WEST: *May the spirits of the Water and Rain Elements look upon and bless this Holy Nemeton, consecrated and dedicated*

> *to the mysteries of the Universe. Nurture and give life while protecting from deluge and fierce storms.*

You may wish to supplement this rite with individual "Tree Awakenings" and various other rites to more intensely "awaken" and "enchant" the land. With repeated use, this Grove portion of the forest will eventually stand apart, noticeable to folk with even the slightest sensitivity, and may even appear more "alive." Such is the nature of true *Elvish Druid Forest Magick!*

rays of light and energy play

According to traditional Bardic and Druid lore, "Three Rays" compose all energetic manifestations, passing through the "Three Spheres"—or great divisions—of Existence. The smallest inner circle is "*Abred,*" which is the physical world, a plane of condensed energy, including the "Green World of Nature." The next sphere is "*Gwynedd,*" the Otherworld—or Astral—which exists as a "higher" spatial dimension that envelopes the physical world. Finally, there is "*Ceugent,*" which is to say "*Nirvana,*" or the "Kingdom of Heaven," where resides the Source-of-All-Being-and-Creation and, in some traditions, those spirits that have achieved "Supreme Ascension"—those who have successfully climbed the "Ladder of Lights" back to the Source.

True Elven Magick—energy work and light-work—requires calling on and using Divine Radiance, which manifests as colored 'Rays' of the Forces of Nature. These auric streams of energy and consciousness are summoned by will, intention and emotion collectively. Once a Wizard has projected awareness into the Light Body, the color of the auric "Light Shield" may be altered to meet a desired energy vibration. Call the energy down as a beam of light from the stars and then allow yourself to assimilate its essence.

The properties of the "Three Rays of Awen" are of Divine or spiritual "silver," "crystalline" and "gold." These are further divided —fragmented or condensed—into the *seven* bands of light. The primary Rays are called upon in Elvish High Magick. Modern practitioners find that identifying the *Rays* by color is a most convenient and accurate way of differentiating their relative degrees on a continuous "spectrum."

The color—and thereby, nature—of one's own "Light Shield" is transformed by the work to match and attract the desired energetic currents. Remember, as you experiment with the *Rays* and light-work, that these various colored degrees are all derived from three primary rays, which in turn are the manifestations of a singularity of *All-ness*. Using visualization and Will, you may call down the radiance of the "Rays" and allow yourself to absorb it through all of your pores and then radiate it from your aura and each breath. Classifications of the *Rays* are as follows:

THE SILVER (LEFT) RAY

Sound/Letter: I ("*ee*")
Polarity: Female, dark, passive, lunar.
Quartile Element: Water (some Earth)
Elvish Element: The Sea
Physical Manifestation: Mineral Kingdom
Threshold Time: Dusk, sunset, autumn.
Elessar (Elf-Stone): Silver (hematite)
Light Bands (Rays): Indigo, violet and blue.

The Silver Properties of the Light Rays

VIOLET (Saturn): Astral vision, darkness, Otherworld work, wisdom, wards.
Domain: Element of Vapor/Cloud
INDIGO (Jupiter): Beauty, enchantment, emotions, love, music, play.
Domain: Element of Rain
BLUE (Luna): Compassion, dreams, healing, peace and understanding.
Domain: Element of Sea

THE GOLD (RIGHT) RAY

Sound/Letter: O ("*oh*")
Polarity: Masculine, light, active, solar.
Quartile Element: Fire and Air
Elvish Element: The Sky
Phys. Manifestation: Animal & Human
  Kingdoms
Threshold Time: Dawn, sunrise,
  spring/summer.
Elessar (Elf-Stone): Gold (tiger's eye)
Light Bands (Rays): Yellow, orange and red.

The Golden Properties of the Light Rays

YELLOW (the Sun): Knowledge, intellect,
              confidence, and inspiration.
              Domain: Element of Skyfire
ORANGE (Mercury): Communication,
              courage, being aware, wishes.
              Domain: Element of Star
RED (Mars): Transformation, healing,
              strength, willpower, and
              leadership.
              Domain: Element of Flame

THE CRYSTALLINE (MIDDLE) RAY

Sound/Letter: A ("*ah*")
Polarity: Neutral, crystalline, reflective
Quartile Element: Earth ('Quintessence.')
Elvish Element: The Land
Physical Manifestation: Plant & Tree
  Kingdom
Threshold Time: Twilight, midnight, winter.
Elessar (Elf-Stone): Black (obsidian) or
  Green
Light Band (Ray): Green

The Crystalline Properties of the Light Ray

GREEN (Venus): Life-force, balance, healing,
        growth, true love.
        Domain: Element of Earth

The traditional "Elven-Faerie Star" is a seven-pointed septogram. Elemental symbolism differs from the "pentagram"—which obviously represents Earth, Air, Fire, Water and *Akasha*. Elvish Wizards see elements as manifestations of Seven Rays of Creation, powers descended from the Source-of-All-Being that make up the myriad of lights that we call manifestation. The Seven Rays also correlate to the traditional "seven energetic centers" of the body—called "calen" and "astyr" or "chakras" in various traditions—all related back to the primary Three Rays and the holistic singularity.

<u>VIOLET RAY—INTERCONNECTEDNESS</u>

Spiritual Element: Fire-of-Spirit (*Nwyvre-of-Akasha*)

Light-Centre: The Crown or Flower of Life (*7th Chakra*)

Gemstone: Amethyst specifically.

A core belief and teaching of Elven Druid Tradition concerns unity of life. Everything shares energetic ties to everything else—and everything is connected together at the "highest" spatial or spiritual plane of existence. Sylvan light-work—such as that which allows a seed to grow faster and stronger—is dependent on a premise that "thought-forms" and emotion have abilities to charge or affect the energy around us. This energy may be focused as a colored *Ray*—filtered with intention and emotion, as if placing a piece of colored film over a white light projection. The energy of the "Violet Ray" is the highest frequency—and shortest wavelength—of all the vibrations treated in this system. As such it should be only used for the highest caliber of mystical work, Ascension work and Transcendental magic—matters involving activation of the "true Self," inner development, "star-walking" and reconnecting with the ALL.

THE PURPLE RAY—THE SEA

Spiritual Element: Water-of-Spirit and Water-of-Earth

Light-Centre: Heart or Merkaba (*4th Chakra*)

Gemstones: Quartz, quicksilver, silver, sapphire, and turquoise.

The Sea is powerful. It is the perfect "liquid" manifestation of the "inter-connectedness" envisioned at the first point. The tides of the Cosmic Sea are the waves of potentiality—they represent the Will and Ability of Cosmic Law in motion. The Sea and Water Elements possess a long-standing association with the Moon and "emotional condition" of our make-up—which bridges the "Mind" with the "physical body," a vast network of energetic communication and exchange. The ebb and flow of these waves of energy manifest as both gentle tides and fierce rushing currents. This "Purple Ray" is called upon to aid in centering and purifying our emotions and, in effect, the proper use of Will and intention. It is the second 'highest' "magick" on the 'Ladder of Lights', by which one can reach a *Self-Honest* experience of life from the Violet rung.

THE BLUE RAY—THE MOON

Spiritual Element: Earth-of-Water and Water-of-Air

Light-Centre: Sex Organs (womb) and Spleen (*2nd Chakra*)

Gemstones: Hematite, Pearl, Topaz and Lapis Lazuli.

Indeed, the Sun is a necessary condition for life derived from light, but the Moon *influences* the beings of light. The ancients believed that the Moon was a luminary body, but of course, we know now that it actually reflects the Sun's light—much like the reflective surface of the Sea. Tidal cycles of water are influenced by a magnetic pull on the earth from the Moon. There are thirteen lunar cycles in a 365-day solar year—and just as many menstrual cycles for a woman. The Moon may affect cyclic psychological, hormonal and behavioral biorhythms on Earth. Different people generally maintain "higher" or "lower" energy levels cycling with different times of day, week, month and year. These patterns are unique to each individual and may be discovered only though self-reflection and self-analysis. The "Blue Ray" is called for perfect peace and protection—such as for casting a Circle of Power. Disruption of the Blue Ray (*2nd Chakra*) causes depression and anxiety—the polar opposites of the peace and security spectrum—and so use of this *Ray* may aid in restoring a personal balance as needed.

THE GREEN RAY—THE WOODLANDS

Spiritual Element: Earth-of-Earth and Earth-of-Air

Light-Centre: Ground (feet) or base of spine (*1st Chakra*)

Gemstones: Amazonite, Aventurine, Emerald, Moss Agate and Serpentine.

An inclination toward the "Green World," and its currents, is the epitome of "Elven Magick." Woodlands and forests are for the Elven-Ffayrie what water is to fish. The "Green Ray" life-force energy is used in all "tree communication rites" and "growth magick." A subversion of the "Green Ray" in its pale (greenish-yellow) form may produce jealousy, envy and discord. When used properly, a Wizard will change their "Light Shield" to match color hues of the forest they are communing with. Trees are the most sacred icon of the "Green Ray"—growing their branches out like the dendritic snowflake, the "Sign of Awen" or the "Elf-rune." Additionally, the "Green Ray" may be used in rites/meditation for personal grounding (centering) and to assist healing.

THE YELLOW RAY—THE SUN

Spiritual Element: Earth-of-Fire, Starfyre and Air-of-Fire

Light-Centre: Mind (Third Eye) or Brow (*6th Chakra*)

Gemstones: Citrine Diamond, Gold, Tiger's Eye and Topaz.

As the Moon is the celestial sphere most sacred to the "Silver Ray," so the Sun brilliantly illuminates the "Golden Ray." All Three Rays of Illumination were once thought to originate with the Sun—which like all other Stars, must originate in the "White Place," a plane of *Infinite Light*. White Light is indicative of the Middle or "Crystalline Ray," and the use of a prism reveals that all Seven Rays are actually contained within one. Crystals may be charged with any *Ray*-color (frequency) or intention through Will and Emotion.

The "Yellow Ray" is called forth in connection to the intellect, mental faculties and the accumulation of wisdom—by whatever class (and color) that may fall under. It is interesting that the "Blue Ray" and "Yellow Ray" on either side of the "Green Ray" also share some of the reflective properties of the Green Ray—and as we know in our experiences with artistic colors: mixing yellow and blue results in green. The Elven-Faerie Star paradigm is quite fluid in this way, demonstrating interconnectivity, *not* separation.

THE ORANGE RAY—THE WINDS

Spiritual Element: Air-of-Air, Air-of-Earth
  and Fire-of-Air
Light-Centre: Throat (Respiratory) or
  Breath (*5th Chakra*)
Gemstones: Amber, Carnelian, Jacinth
  and Opal.

Winds are particularly sacred to the Sylph-
Ffayrie types. It is the power of the Air Element, with warm currents driven by the
Sun, that blows seeds containing the spark
of life ensuring the continuation of Nature.
Powers of the breeze or wind element are
often overlooked because they are represented by the most intangible and unseen
symbols—but reflect some of the strongest
manifestations of energy in motion. When
the wind is "at your back," in may help
carry you further. If blowing in the proper
direction, in may aid in delivering clear
communication at a distance. Otherwise,
the "Orange Ray" is only used to relay information that you *really* want to stand out
and draw attention to. Next to red, it carries the longest-wavelength, and demands

attention, which is why so many in positions of leadership radiate orange in their "Light Shield."

THE RED RAY—THE MAGICK

Spiritual Element: Fire-of-Fire and Spirit-of-Fire

Light-Centre: Solar Plexus (stomach) (*3rd Chakra*)

Gemstones: Red Jasper, Red Agate, Ruby and Rose Quartz.

Practical Magick—such as the "Elementalism" introduced earlier in this *Elvenomicon* series, in the "*Elven-Faerie Grimoire*" volume —is often a *seeker's* first step on the path to clearing and defragmenting the programs of the "Mind-system" and the Reality experience of the Human condition.

Ritual-magic and similar forms of ceremonial practice may aid the novice in understanding and developing their own abilities —but we must make sure that we do not falsely attribute power to these "rituals" themselves, and that we do not fall into the trap of over-identifying with the ritualism or dependent on such "external" forms as our only means of thinking and acting "magically." All truly intentional actions—or movements of energy intended from the true Will—performed deliberately are considered "magical," and only when a true conscious understanding of these principles and dynamics becomes automatic second-nature to us, do we begin to say that we are practicing or operating "magick."

Much more than rituals and spells, degrees of initiation or fancy dress, the purpose of the magical pursuits is to engage on a specific process or pathway—a progressive journey toward active participation as *Self* in *Self-Honesty* with Cosmic Law of the ALL—and these are not affirmations of someone who lives life only in response or as a victim, no indeed, we are actively creating with the "Red Ray" and it manipulates the emotional states of passion, consummate love and anger—currents with the longest wave and most immediate tangible results.

communing
with nature

Prior to working with the entire spectrum, an initiate might begin their journey into "Light Work" or "Energy Work" with the "Three Rays of Radiance." The following "Triad Rite" assists with this. Once a basic familiarity with the system is reached, Rites of the Rays may be performed anywhere—in a physical setting or purely while working on the 'astral' or 'mental' plane—and always from the perspective of *Self* within an activated "Light Body."

THREE RAYS OF RADIANCE
"THE TRIAD RITE"

• Face the northern direction.
• Call down the Radiance of the "Silver Ray."
• See and feel the "Silver Ray" descend upon you, and to the left of you, as you intone the sound "I" ("ee").
• Raise your arms as you inhale the tone; bringing them down to your

sides as you exhale and intone the sound—using your arms to draw or pull down the "air" (*Ray*).

- Do this with the Middle or "Crystalline Ray."

- See and feel the "Crystalline Ray" descending upon you, and through you, with the sound "A" ("*ah*").

- Repeat the process, calling the "Golden Ray" down upon you, and to the right of you, with the intonation "O" ("*oh*").

- With practice, the rite may conclude by drawing down all "Three Rays" using the three processes simultaneously: "I-A-O."

- You might also try experimenting with other Elven sequences, such as "A-O-I."

Elven lore includes many references to an "Astral Grove" and "astral plane"—suggesting this environment as most suitable for meditation and ritual work. But this is only available to those with proficiency in accessing such state of consciousness.

To assist in this development, there is an effective exercise—called "A Day at the Pool"—that 'New Age' teachers offer their students to practice directing (projecting) mental energy in an 'astral', 'mental' or otherwise imagined universe.

Try this:—Enter the Body of Light and begin first at your Astral Grove, asking for the grace of the Cosmic Source to protect your Beingness as you work. Now travel through the "Everlasting Astral Forest" until you find a still pool or lake—making certain you are experiencing all of the sensory details of your surroundings as you move through this fluid-like degree of existence: the colors; smells; the feeling of the ground beneath your feet...

Then begin to practice your intentional interaction with the environment—drawing in energy (inhale through your astral form) to make deliberate movements and actions with the Astral Body. For, example, extend the energy with an exhale as you bend down to pick up a rock from the waters edge. Hold it a while, feeling it completely in your hands, making certain the imagery is concrete as you build your Will and to focus. Continue to perform simple actions, tossing the rock from one hand to the other, inhaling energy and exhaling action. Then use your will (and exhale) as you cast the stone across the still waters of the pond —releasing and projecting energy. Pause a moment to witness the results. Did you see ripples across the pond as consequence of the energy you directed? [This type of exercise may be repeated as desired for cumulative experience.]

To summon the Radiance of peace and protection about yourself—or to a specific locale—conjure a "ball" of compressed blue-white energy rays between your hands. Feel its radiance warming and cooling your hands simultaneously. It may help if you perform a "Triad Rite" first and call on the "Blue Ray" directly as you construct the "ball." Use the "Three Rays" to give the ball substance, then incorporate the "Blue Ray" to provide its "shield" or energetic filter.

If this does not work for you at first, try rubbing your hands back and forth together repeatedly while initially drawing down the

Radiance, and then bring them apart several inches and focus your energy and attention on the space between your hands. When the ball is adequately visualized and experienced, feel the "*Radix*" or "*Rad*" of the ball emanating out, affecting the surrounding environment with its radiation, driving all out-of-phase frequencies and negative conditions away. Then direct the "positive" Radiance of the ball toward a target, or absorb it internally. This practice is otherwise known as a "*Blessing*."

We have mentioned Light Shields of living systems (beings) in passing—but these same "auric covers" exist for all things. They are the "energetic frequency signature" of that "thing"—fragmented from the Unmanifest as a "thing" in exclusion to "other things"— a filtering determinant of the energy projected and received by that existence and in relation to other existences.

Colored bands associated with living beings are consequences of energetic activity moving through the body on all degrees/levels of existence. These colors may typically distinguish what energy type is most actively projecting into the field. Each color carries frequencies associated with basic attributes that may be either "under-stimulated" or "over-active"—with the ability to generate "positive" constructive frequencies in our daily life and work, or "negative" wave-interference patterns. The choice is ours.

Understand that we are not here speaking in absolutes—"good" and "evil"—but, what we *have* discovered is that there are modes of operation (thought and activity) that contribute either *toward* or *away from* progression on our "Path of Ascension." These also tend to solidify or manifest in our daily lives and directly relate to spiritual evolution, emotional well-being and yes, even our physical health—all of which is interconnected; nothing treated is in exclusion.

There is nothing wrong with treating physical ailment symptoms with physical medicine as a tool that might enable the "Mind" and "Spirit" to focus on its own degrees of health. But when we focus on the physical ailments and remedies in exclusion, the underlying "problems" continue to resurface.

Esoteric lore from the "Ancient Mystery School" also alludes to the existence of the colors and Rays in descriptions of the degrees/levels of existence that make up the total identity of *Self* as it came to be more locatable in time-space (with the successive condensation of universes). It states that: at the innermost core of your being there is a "violet egg" or oval-like elliptical sphere containing the essence of your True Spirit. All of the rest—all the other bands and layers—are further and further shells that resonate increasingly condensed degrees of existence. This includes our "biochemical" genetic vehicle that the Spirit calls "home" for its earthly condition of experience.

Elven-Faerie lore describes a "violet egg" as "amethyst" (or violet quartz)—and that it is a "fragmented shard" of a now "Dark Crystal," something that seems to resonate with a certain brand of modern-day fantasy. The "amethyst crystal" of our True Spirit is protected in an encasement of spiritual skin—a pink shell that radiates the true love and absolute purity of the ALL. This violet-pink hued spiritual existence is the truest part of our spiritual identity, which came from and may return to the Source—the destination of Ascension called "*Ceugent*" in Welsh literature.

This true spiritual state is the connection link back to the Source—a column that is aligned directly with the "Middle Ray" or "Crystalline Ray" (from which both the "Silver Ray" and "Golden Ray" divert) that activates our personal energetic propulsion system (that some call *chakras*) as an "Identity"—the light centers that are anchored to us and within us that align to variously perceived degrees/levels that project our more material existence—and our ability to simultaneously exist—at all degrees/levels of the ALL at once. Without such a function, we would have no consciousness, no ability to relate to our created environment, and no memory to retain either across time and space—and all past spiritual lifetimes.

When the white crystalline energy of the Light Body has stabilized (equalized) or is "clear," it is then able to manifest all colors of the spectrum perfectly. These Rays use the body's *Chakra-system*—or "*Calen*" system —as an energetic "step-down transformer" connected to "Divine" Radiance of the Cosmos. According to lore: the fourth level of your "etheric body" consists of both a silver and a gold shell that wraps around the crystalline one, sealing primary auric energy in as part of the spiritual identity (independent of any body). The fifth level is the 'Light Body' itself—"outer aura" or "Light Shield." It is the part that people may see when they say they "see auras." Energetic and emotional states influence the type, nature and strength of the auric "Light Shield"—and *vice versa*, because all energetic activity is also an exchange (or communication).

It is possible to neutralize negative or destructive aspects of an emotion (color) by changing the "Light Shield"—and therefore conscious attention—to an opposing color. For example—a person might counter the "red" they see when angry with "blue" peaceful hues. When we meditate on the nature of this multiplicity of oneness that we perceive as levels of the "spiritual self," we may strengthen our abilities to consciously interact with these energies as a part of a daily holistic practice.

The same systems of consciousness and energetic interaction we apply to ourselves is also present in other forms of life—including animals and trees. Therefore, it is important that an initiate is first aware of how this energetic systems operates on *themselves* before attempting to interact, commune, or otherwise exchange energies directly with Nature or other living systems—and specifically the *trees* that the remainder of this "grimoire" is focused on.

Tree Magick is a uniquely personal form of mystic practice used by Elven-Faerie Wizards—and later Druids—to awaken the individual consciousness of trees on Earth, one by one. These awakened trees form groups or "chains," composing a complex network of communication—and energetic exchange —with the other awakened or "Enchanted" trees. Through "high magical" processes of "Communion with Nature," an Elven-Faerie Wizard or Druid is capable of learning otherwise untold spiritual lessons from Nature and awakened tree-spirits, because they are all linked to the planetary pool of "Earth Memory," just as each of us is influenced by encoded genetic memory within the design of these mortal body-shells that may even be billions of years old.

An advanced use of these abilities might include activating a ring of awakened trees to guard (monitor) an area around your home. Linking with the Forces of Nature, a sensitive adept may notice when the surrounding area has a "visitor" or is disturbed—like the strings of a spider's web. Other more abstract practices could include accessing data from the Elven Libraries—what some refer to as "Akashic Records."

The Forest Magickal Tradition is so vast and colorful that entire lifetimes could be dedicated to its ways and unlimited applications. To "Commune with Nature," any skills developed from previous exercises in Visualization and Willpower will be tested. The following are prerequisite steps of the traditional "Commune with Nature" spell-rite before performing any other specific acts.

  • Go to the sacred woods where you practice your art of energy-play and light-weaving. This will most likely be the *Nemeton* ('magic circle' or 'grove') or place where you most often spend time developing your magical arts.

• Spend some time meditating on the "Elven-Faerie Tradition" or Druidry.

• Project your awareness into your "Light Body."

• Adjust or tune your "Light Body" to match the green energy vibrations of the woodlands.

• Use muscular inclination ("Dowsing-With-Your-Feet") to guide you to a specific tree (assuming it is one that is not a part of the 'grove' or have not already selected). [At first you may want to work with only a few tree types—but eventually you may be able to awaken the entire forest.]

• When working with individual trees, approach slowly and from the north (when possible) and with a quieted "mind." Do not bring a head full of cluttered worldly matters to your Elven Green World energy-work.

• Sit close—within an arm's reach— and focus on both your "Light Shield" and the "auric radiation" of the *tree*.

• Spread your palms wide on the surface of the trunk.
• Match your frequency and vibration (color) with the tree and then merge the two energy fields.
• Retain contact with your left hand, completing the circuit with your right hand by using some catalyst for the energy—such as sticks, stones or the ground, depending on your other intended practices.

Now that the preliminaries are performed, what follows will depend on what type of 'Green Magick' you have intended. Not all Nature-communion sessions are for literal "communication." Basic communion is the first step regardless.

Visualize—and maintain an awareness—of a clear circuit of energy. The pillared trunk of the tree represents the "Tower of the Green Ray," the Middle Ray of pure crystalline reflection. Take this energy into your circulatory and nervous system through your left (or receptive) hand spread on the trunk. Make it a part of you, then send it forth to the ground (after cycling it through your catalyst or tool)—just as you would an electric circuit! The root structure of the tree takes this energy in, circulates it through its own internal nervous system—passing through trunk, branch and sprig—before it is passed back to you.

When both aspects ('terminals') are sending and receiving simultaneously, there is no energy "drain." When life-force energies are cycled, they are filtered as a result of the process, which may be beneficial when it is clear *Self-Honest* filtering—much like removing corrosion from a wire-connection or electrical contact. Such exchanges also take place during sexual encounters: energy is projected and permanently changes by the "energetic signature" of a partner, and then returns. When we engage in such activities without understanding energy peroperly, there is a risk of damaging or depleting auric energy from our "*chakra-system*" and/or "Light Bodies."

Once you commune, you can communicate: —Close your eyes and see a whitish etheric "cloud" between you and the tree, slightly above your head. Both of you share this 'field' and have the ability to project into it. Understand: trees are not verbal "talkers." They prefer—and are mostly restricted—to communicate in the timeless language of symbols and imagery; hence, in this case, a "picture *is* worth a thousand words."

So long as true communion exists between you and Nature, the verbal use of communication—for example, in rites and rituals—are mainly for your benefit, and to assist focus on actual communicable energy transmissions. Members of the animal and plant kingdom are more likely to hear and respond to tone and "emotional charge" (or your Light Body resonance) than the words themselves. Use the "cloud" previously described as a "thought-bubble" to facilitate communication. Then wait and be patient to see what happens. Tree communication is often slow work—even for an adept.

The Elven Forest Magick system is loosely aligned to the later Druidic classification of *Ogham* trees—a "systemology" derived from the former—and explored in more depth in "*Book of Ogham*" (also in this series).

There are three different traditional sets of "*Ogham Tools*" that are often all haphazardly referred to as "*Ogham Sticks*." Elven tradition gives each of the versions its own title and each are kept separately in their own magical pouch—called a "Crane Bag" in the *Oghamic* tradition and system.

OGHAM STICKS—Twenty sticks/twigs of the same type/species, cut to the same size and polished. An alternate version uses woodchips as "runic wood-stones." Each stick or chip will have one of the Ogham glyphs burned (preferably), cut or painted thereon. "Ogham Sticks" are used for high-divination and "cryptomancy."

OGHAM WANDS—Ranging from eight to sixteen inches long, each wand should be constructed from the correlating tree for each Ogham sign if possible—or a tree of similar energy. The "handle" of the wand should be shaved flat on one side so there is a surface to burn or paint an Ogham sign. The other end should be sanded or filed to a stake-like or spear-like point so it may be pushed several inches into the ground. During communion or communication, the Elven Wizard holds the handle of the wand to complete the energetic circuit. "Ogham Wands" are primarily used for communication and spiritual communion with Nature.

<u>OGHAM RODS</u>—Twenty-one pieces of dowel or thin wood that are cut to equal lengths and used specifically for divination. Some scholars suggest this ancient tool set inspired the game "pick-up-sticks"—which is what an objective observer might see when the set of rods is cast, interpreted and retrieved. "Ogham rods" are held in one hand about a foot or so away from the ground, and then dropped. Using runic and Ogham signs as reference, the Wizard may interpret any omens found or "read."

When used in conjunction with tree communication and communion with Nature, even simple acts of "divination" may become powerful workings of "Elven High Forest Magick." The "*Elf Stones*" are another perfect example of this.

<u>ELF-STONES</u>—(*Elessar*)—are among the most sacred tools of "Sylvan Magick." They may be used for any purpose: divination, tree

communication and various energy-work. Elven lore suggests many different versions —including all-blue and all-green sets—but always sets of three stones.

"Triscale Oracle Stones" are the most commonly described in traditional Celtic lore— three equal-sized stones, each tapping into the energetic heart of one of the "Three Rays of Radiance" or Elven "*Awen*."

> "Golden Ray" — Tiger's Eye
> "Silver Ray" — Hematite
> "Crystalline Ray" — Obsidian*

"Elf Stones" are a perfect catalyst for divination and tree communication, acting as a an energy-testor, similar to the function of a "pendulum" or "dowsing rods." A standard "Triscale Set" may be used to indicate 'positive' or 'negative' responses (answers) based on where the gold and silver stone fall in relation to the black/green crystalline indicator stone.

---

*   Some sets substitute aventurine or bloodstone for the obsidian.

To use the Elf-Stones in relation to "Tree Magick," you might try the following:—Link up to a tree energy from your Light Body and ask it if it is in need of a Guardian and Caretaker or if it wishes to begin a mystical and spiritual relationship with you. Drop the stones at the base of the tree and see how they fall. If the gold one is closest to the indicator, the answer is "yes." The answer is "no" if the silver stone is closer.

Practices related to 'Ogham Tools' and 'Elf-Stones' are all great for developing skills of "Elven High Forest Magick," but they are dependent on sensitivity and awareness of a practitioner for effectiveness. More information on these is found in our "*Book of Ogham*"—another title in this series. Such tools (and techniques) formerly described may also assist in "Awakening the Forest." In fact, one of the final rites offered in the original "Greenwood Forest Grimoire" is a direct suggestion to accomplish just that:—

ELVEN-DRUID HIGH FOREST MAGICK
"THE TREE AWAKENING"

- Enter your "Light Body."
- Call down the "Radiance of the Three Rays."
- Make physical contact with the tree.
- Perform the "Tree Communion" spell.
- Speak the "Elven-Gaelic name" for the tree species three times, followed by the "English name," and finally the names "Aldaron," "Daghda" and the "Guardian-name" (associated with the type/species).
- Knock three times and break contact.
- The tree is *awakened!*

tbe "great tree" rite

The 'Great Tree Rite' first carried an exclusively lunar-orientation—used for Full Moon observances and complimenting the solar orientation of the traditional "Grove Festivals" marking the annual 'Wheel'. It may, of course, be also added to solar rituals used during these seasonal observances—such as those found in *"The Elven-Faerie Grimoire."*

This ritual text follows the same "elemental alignment" as other rites in the *Elvenomicon* series; and similarly, while originally written for group applications, may be modified for use by solitary practitioners. As a "rite" it is generally added to other magical and ritual work. It honors the 'Sacred Tree' of the Grove—one that is generally included in the 'Magic Circle' itself.

THE GREAT TREE RITE

<u>Leader</u>: *We are here to give witness to the unity and strength of the magic circle, this mandala of love most holy. We, the Druids, the Children of Light, are at one with thee, Oh Sacred Tree. You, who stands as an eternal symbol of the*

Circle of Light and Life. You, who represent our eternal link with the ever-present Source. We honor and imitate you as the perfect living specimen of the Source of All Being and Creation. We watch you as you progress through the sacred Earth Year.

<u>North</u>: *The beginnings, middles, and ends of the sacred Earth Year.*

<u>East</u>: *The balanced forces and equinox equalities of the sacred Earth Year.*

<u>South</u>: *Tonight (today) we coven together, humans and tree, acknowledging the Sacred Grove.*

<u>West</u>: *We celebrate the strength, love, and unity of the Sacred Grove, and in that celebration we honor the central icon of its existence: The Great Tree.*

<u>East</u>: *From the Eastern Winds we are granted a season of growth, as the sun emerges in the spring.*

<u>South</u>: *From the Southern Flame we are granted a season of fullness, as the sun warms the summer.*

<u>West</u>: *From the Western Waves we are granted*

a season of transformation with the shifting tides of autumn.

<u>North</u>: *From the Firmness of Northern Ground we are granted a season of stability, self-reflection, and stillness, as the Earth hibernates and is renewed through winter.*

<u>Leader</u>: *The calendrical month ___, the Oghamic month of the ___ tree in the ancient Druid's calender.* [Traces an appropriate Ogham sign in the air. Then continues.] *May the blessing of ___, and the corresponding energies of ___ be projected forth into our auric light.*

GREAT TREE RITE—OGHAMIC KEYS

January: Alder Tree, *Fearn*, F, protection and power.
February: Willow Tree, *Saille*, S, healing and enchantment.
March: Ash Tree, *Nuin*, N, protection and peace.
April: Hawthorn Tree, *Huatha*, H, love and purity.
May: Oak Tree, *Duir*, D, strength and leadership.

June: Holly, *Tinne*, T, purification and balance.

July: Hazel Tree, *Coll*, C, intuition and creativity.

August: Vine, *Muin*, M, meditation and prophecy.

September: Ivy, *Gort*, G, protection and growth.

October: Reed, *Ngetal*, Ng, intense energy and direct action.

13th:[*] Elder Tree, *Ruis*, R, completion and reflection. Alternatively: Yew.

November: Birth Tree, *Beith*, B, fertility and new growth.

December: Rowan Tree, *Luis*, L, strength and insight.

Winter Solstice: Silver Fir, *Ailim*, A, objectivity and longevity.

Spring Equinox: Furze/Gorse, *Ohn*, O, fertility and inspiration.

Summer Solstice: Heather, *Ur*, U, healing and support.

Autumn Equinox: Aspen, *Eadha*, E, ascension and immortality.

---

[*] *13th Month*—A "*Blue Moon*" or Samhain or the three days leading up to a '*New Year*' observation.

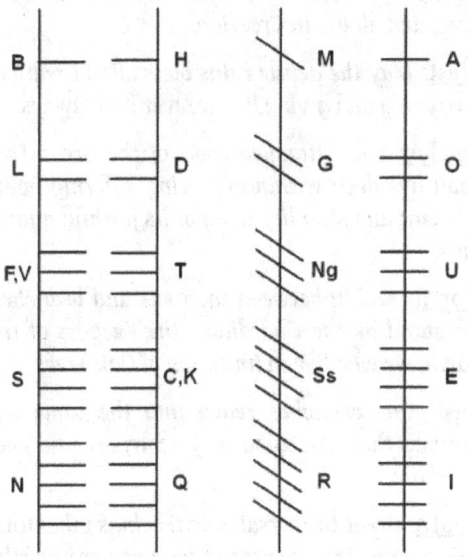

The Traditional Celtic-Druid Ogham

East: *May the Sacred Grove and the Great Tree grant us the strength of the ancient Druids.*

South: *We hereby swear (reaffirm) our Guardianship of Gaea, the Sacred Grove, the Great Tree, and all life in Creation.*

West: *May the gentle rains bless all of Creation, nurturing and giving life, forever and always.*

Leader: *The entangled roots of the Great Tree shall live deep within our being, offering nourishment and stability to all of its faithful guardians.*

North: *And in between the roots and branches, we stand as the Guardians, the Keepers of the Earth, we who live in imitation of Oak Trees.*

East: *Our branches reach into the same sky proving that ascension is the purpose and goal of all life.*

South: *Great Universal Spirit, beings inhabiting this Sacred Tree, we stand here as your worthy guardians, and Keepers of the Earth and her mysteries.*

West: *May we grow to become our full potential from the seedlings we now are. May seeds plant in the world, bloom and flourish, spreading the* *true beauty and love of the Source of All, shared by all those receptive.*

<u>Leader</u>: [Traces appropriate Ogham sign on the tree; knocks three times lightly on the trunk, intoning names of the tree (often the English, Elvish-Celtic and Guardian names) with each knock. Then continues.] *Oh Great Tree, you are hereby awakened by the Druids of the ancient and ineffable knowledge.*

<u>North</u>: *May the ground that covers the roots, forever and always be blessed with all that is good and holy. May all of creation grow as the trees in the forest, each beautiful in their own uniqueness, yet still sharing the same Earth in which too spread roots and call home.*

<u>Leader</u>: *We are united in our strengths, our faith, our love, and our trust. Ours in the bond that must endure all other bonds. The Truth Against the World.*

<u>All</u>: *The Truth Against The World.*

<u>Leader</u>: *Through True Knowledge, Power.*

<u>All</u>: *Through True Knowledge, Power.*

<u>Leader</u>: *So mote it be.*

by wand, ward and staff

The Druid Wand and Wizard Staff—called *"slatan drui'echt"* (literally: magic rod, wand or staff)—are iconic symbols of magic; and when made of wood, they represent a wizard's relationship with the woodlands and trees. Each is believed to contain the very essence of the *dryad* spirit that inhabits the tree—thus a regimen of reverently extracting a sacred wood specimen only after magically awakening a tree, asking its permission and doing as little damage as possible in the process. A cutting ceremony should also be performed, which includes casting a circle around the donor-tree and wizard.

Additional lore on the magical properties of each individual wood-type or tree (and suggestions of use as *wands* or *wards*) is found in the next section ('Sylvan Druieachd'). For the moment, we will simply distinguish the types of tools, themselves, which are described and/or referred to throughout this book—and greater body of the *Elvenomicon*.

WAND—a thin branch (half to three-quarters of an inch thick or so—although thickness often varies along its length) used as a focusing tool for directing 'streams' or 'currents' of energy—via attention—in 'ritual magic'. In Elven-Faerie tradition a *wand* is representative of the Air element and the action that is transmitted via thought.

WARD—a wand-like branch (usually four to sixteen inches long and decoratively crafted) used (or hung) as a 'talisman'—or protective magical artifact—to *ward* away certain energies. *Wards* are derived from Celtic lore, where an Elvish Wizard or Druid performs "magic" (called '*druieachd*' or '*druidecht*') by cutting or carving symbols on a branch and reciting a "spell." Some traditions refer to the *ward* as a '*rod*'. A longer (*staff*) version is often called a '*stave*'—from which we get the expression to "stave off" something. Interestingly, a '*stave*' is a name for a 'rung' on a ladder, and also a 'stanza' from Bardic poetry.

STAFF—a thicker longer branch, resembling a 'walking stick'—with medium-length ones often called '*rods*'. A staff is essentially a large vertical wand that maintains an axis connecting land and sky—or else the polarity of the seen and unseen, the material and the spiritual, or else *Beta-Existence* contrasting with the truer *Alpha* reality (if we are to include systemological terms). In the Elven-Faerie tradition, the *staff* or *rod* is typically representative of the Fire element—a symbol of the force and authority (presumably of Will) that is exercised by the wizard.

Now that we have established what is traditional, it should be noted that these 'rules' are not "dogma." As an example: lore suggests specific rules for sizing a wand—such as using the length of your elbow to palm, or elbow to fingertip, &tc. The truth is that a wand will either feel comfortable and natural when held by an individual, or it won't. And while traditionalists support extracting wand and staff wood from living trees, this is not an absolute rule either. Many fine tools have been crafted from branches of fallen trees and even store-bought wood.

Each wand and staff you construct is individually named during its dedication rite or consecration ceremony.

Additional details for consecrating tools as given in the Elven-Faerie tradition may be found in "*The Elven-Faerie Grimoire*" volume of this series.

Elsewhere in occult lore, the *Key of Solomon* instructs that the ceremonial staff should be constructed of 'elderwood', or 'cane' or 'rosewood'; and the wand from 'hazel' or a nut-tree—but made from "*virgin-wood.*"

This term 'virgin-wood' is ambiguous and was once thought to mean: from a tree of one year's growth only that had not budded (or fruited). Anyone that has actually seen such a tree would probably not find it suitable for staff wood. It is more likely that the phrase indicates a tree that has not been previously cut on for any other purpose—but that is only a theory.

Much like a '*caduceus*' indicative of Hermes, the wand and staff is "sacred" (or 'aligned') to the planet Mercury. Therefore, the traditional time to cut or construct one is the "day and hour of Mercury"—which is to say Wednesday at dawn. Some of the common staff-wand types in Celtic lore include:

Darkwand/Darkstaff = Blackthorne
Goldwand/Goldstaff = Oak
Silverwand/Silverstaff = Apple
Whitewand/Whitestaff = Hawthorne
Witchwand = Willow or Rowen
Wizardwand/Worldstaff = Ash or Rowen

There is one other archaic tool from Celtic lore worthy of mention here: the "Druid's Rod" is little used among modern revivals, but this ancient tool was often created and carried by an *Ovydd* for their solitary rites during a probation period spent studying and meditating in the woodlands, among the company of trees. Technically, it is two rods connected by a cord, resembling a larger version of the familiar *nunchuk* weapon.

The two rods are attached with a cord so that when the tool is outstretched, there is a rod at each end with the cord between. By fixing one portion in the ground and using the other to trace the boundaries of a nemeton (or ritual circle), the Druid's Rod acts like a drawing compass. The tool could also be arranged to form a sun-dial. As such, it represents a mastery of cosmic knowledge, particularly regarding 'space-time'.

The "Druid's Rod" employs another important facet of little-known Druidic lore, called the 'Megalithic Yard' (abbreviated "MY"). A 'Megalithic Yard' is equivalent to 2.72 feet (which some modern practitioners simply round off to 3-feet). The complete "Druid's Rod" is composed of three measured parts, each 2.72 (or 3) feet long, making the total length approximately 9 feet, or 8.16 if using the strict 'Megalithic Yard'.

SYLVAN
DRUIEACHD

alder tree

Elvish-Celtic Name: Fearn, Gwernen
Ogham Letter: "F"
Druid Guardian: Forann
Archetypes & Deities: Strength, Bran
  the Blessed, Deirdre and Macha.
Quadratic Element: Fire
  Subordinate Element: Water
Colour: Crimson (*'flann'*)
Polarity: Male (solar)
Month of Cor Anar: January
Sacred Animal/Bird: Fox, Ram/
  Gull (*'faelin'*) and Ravens
Gemstones: Beryl, Serpentine and the
  Gold Elf-Stone.
Ffayrie Herb(s): Fern
Traditional Uses: Charcoal, shields,
  dye, and housing foundations.
Divinatory & Energy Expressions:
Foundation, protection, guidance
  (oracular, seership), resistance to
  water/enchantment (preservation).

Oghamic lore attributes the Alder Tree to
the Fire element; yet, additional investiga-
tions into its mysteries reveal that it also
carries an affinity for water—because Alder

wood holds up quite well against it and is capable of actually living in water. For this reason, fortified villages floating on logs in Scotland and many "water-towns" (such as Venice) are built on piles and stilts of Alder wood. Since the Water element and magic of enchantment and glamour are closely related, Alder *wards* away (protects against) such enchantment from others. Due to its unique aquatic growth ability, it represents a bridge or link between the material world and the Otherworld—and, of course, it used to build "bridges" in general.

One clear indicator to the ancients that this is a sacred Faerie-tree is that when it is first cut, it appears as though it were bleeding. Such omens forced wizards to consider that this wood should not be often cut, and so there is a mystical taboo or "*geas*" concerning its use—though it is still often used. It allegedly makes good charcoal and the bark yields a blood-red dye. Fresh shoots produce a more cinnamon-hued dye.

The Fire element and red attributes apply to its use in battle. According to the "*Cad Goddeu*"—"Battle of the Trees"—Alders are at the head of the battle—"first in the foray"—right there on the front line. Warriors often sought Alder wood for their shields.

The blood-like sap is equally reminiscent of wounds in battle—such as those endured by Bran-the-Blessed. Alder energy drives the warrior spirit, allowing one to stand fast in battle or conflict, or when confronted with an overabundance of external pressures. Just as the head of Bran arrived in the midst of battle to reveal important prophecies, so must an Elven Wizard or Druid be open to hearing their own inner voice at all times.

Alder '*wards*' are highly effective. Of course, to obtain Wizardwood, you must touch the tree with a blade, which is taboo except by the most adept of Elven Wizards. Ask the *dryad* spirit of the tree to enter the *ward* and aid safeguarding against the will, magic and enchantment from others toward you, your family—or for the owner of the ward.

Alder is sometimes used for medicinal purposes. The inner bark may be boiled in vinegar and used to anoint the skin to remedy various skin conditions, it tightens gums when used as a mouthwash (or soothes a toothache) and has even been used to help kill head lice and assist with scalp recovery afterward. [As with any "folk medicine" discussed within these pages, the present author suggests the reader/seeker embark on extensive investigation into all homeopathic and holistic medicine—including discussion with a health care professional—before self-treating with any natural suggestions.]

apple tree

Elvish-Celtic Names: Quert, Queris, Afal

Ogham Letter: "Q"

Druid Guardian: Qualep

Archetypes & Deities: The Empress, Avalon, Rhiannon, Pwyll, Arthur, Kerridwen (or Cerridwen) and Mannan Mac Lyr.

Quadratic Element: Water
Subordinate Element: Air

Colour: Green (*'quair'*)

Polarity: Female (lunar)

Sacred Animal/Bird: Unicorn/ Hen (*'querc'*)

Gemstones: Rose Quartz and the Silver Elf-Stone.

Ffayrie Herb(s): Wild Strawberry and Rosebush ('*quenda*')

Traditional Uses: Dietary (fruit) major food of the Elves, drinking (cider,) woodcarving, the "Silver Branch" ("Silver Bough") or "Apple Wand."

Divinatory & Energy Expressions: Love, beauty, the union of mind and spirit between lovers, doorways to other worlds, eternal life (perpetual youth), abundance, spirit calling, fertility and healing.

Many Celtic scholars interpret the name of the ancient *Isle of Affalon* (or "Avalon") as the "Isle of Apples"—also known as the "Isle of Glass" and today, Glastonbury. The Apple Tree and Avalon both share a peculiar connection to the Elven-Ffayrie Otherworld. An examination of ancient lore and references to Avalon suggest it was called "Appleland" —and most likely home to a large orchard or elaborate arrangement of Apple groves. It is said to aid in perceiving other 'worlds'.

An Order—or secret society—of priestesses and Druidesses maintained a mystical tradition in Avalon sacred to the Silver Ray and using Apple Wand in their ceremonies. The *Craebh Ciuil* wand or "Silver Bough" is used for healing, beauty, peace and harmony, in addition to Otherworld Magick. The "Apple Branch" is also a central tool to several magick rites that summon or call the *Fey*. Lore suggests that it is a forked branch, unpainted, with three silver bells hanging on white, silver and/or blue ribbon.

Another reason Apple is sacred is that when the fruit is cut in half, you can see the image of the pentagram—the five-rayed star. *Quert* is sacred to the harvest, festivals of Lughnassadh and the Autumn Equinox. The tree flowers white blossoms near Beltane. A toast of cider is always conducted in the honor of the Apple Tree Spirits at the beginning of the harvest to bless and consecrate the harvest season. The tradition of wassailing occurs during the winter season. All dietary use of Apple hybrids now common first emerged from the original Crab Apple tree—for which the Celtic Ogham letter is named. The also fruit appears in folk remedies for soothing asthma or for chronic pneumonia sufferers—possibly inspiring the old saying that: "...*an apple a day keeps the doctor away.*"

ash tree

Elvish-Celtic Names: Nuin, Nwyn, Nion, Unnen
Ogham Letter: "N"
Druid Guardian: Nebgadon
Archetypes & Deities: The World/Universe, World Tree, Lugh, Ogma, Odin/Woden, Artemis and Diana.
Quadratic Element: Air
  Subordinate Elements: Earth & Water
Colour: Green or Clear (*'necht'*)
Polarity: Crystalline (reflective)
Month of Cor Anar: March
Sacred Animal/Bird: Adder or Serpent/Snipe (*'naescu'*)
Gemstones: Sapphire and the Green or Crystalline Elf-Stone.
Ffayrie Herb(s): Magic Mushroom (*'fly agaric'* in Europe or *'psilocybin'*)
Traditional Uses: Spears, maypoles, pool cues, paddles, oars, hockey

sticks, wands, dream pillow herbs,
sea/water magick and healing.
Divinatory & Energy Expressions:
Triumph, completion, overview,
protection, overcoming mental
strife, and the 'World Tree' that
links the inner and outer worlds
(crossings to the Otherworld).

There are three main wands of the Sylvan
Faerie Druid Tradition—excluding the Silver
(Apple) Branch formerly mentioned—
and they are: Oak, Ash and Thorn. While
Drwyds are best known for their Oak wands,
the legendary Spear of Lugh was fashioned
from Ash wood. The first Elven wands were
possibly of the *Nuin* current, in imitation of
this spear, and often carved into a spiral,
like a Unicorn's horn—always representative
of the Air Element. Ogham tools constructed
from Ash wood are used for inspiration,
enlightenment and most obviously,
knowledge.

Ash is the most likely candidate for a "Tree
of Knowledge" or "World Tree" (*Yggdrasil*)
often referred to in Nordic-Elven lore—or
even the Semitic Kabbalah, which is based

on Mesopotamian lore of the *date-palm* as the "World Tree" or "Tree of Life." In all of its forms, the "World Tree" is a holistic microcosmic-macrocosmic representation or Cosmic model—its branches representing different degree/levels of existence (or dimensions) yet still a part of the singular Tree. Elves sometimes refer to the "Middle World"—or "physical plane" experienced by the Human condition—as "Mid-Branch."

As one of the few truly crystalline tree currents, Ash trees possess the ability to be one sex and then switch based on reproductive needs. According to folk remedy lore, Ash bark may assist in reducing fevers; and the leaves may be used to remove bio-toxins as a laxative, or externally to treat snakebites. When leaves are unavailable (or out of season), the bark is often used with similar results and the sap is sometimes added to teas and infusions to aid relieving kidney stones and bladder infections.

aspen tree

Elvish-Celtic Names: Eadha, Aethin, K'emmir, Poplysen Gwyn

Ogham Letter: "E"

Druid Guardian: Essu

Archetypes & Deities: The Tower,
   Brighid, Rhiannon, Arianrhod,
   Keyne, Proteus and Psyche.

Quadratic Element: Water

Colour: Silver or Red (*'erc'*)

Polarity: Female (lunar)

Other Trees Sharing the Current:
   Poplar & Cottonwood

Sacred Animal/Bird: White Mare/
   Swan (*'ela'*)

Gemstones: Grey Topaz, Opal and the
   Silver Elf-Stone.

Ffayrie Herb(s): Bracken

Traditional Uses: Shapeshifting
   magick, divination, shields and Rites
   of Passage.

Divinatory & Energy Expressions:
   Overcoming barriers and problems,
   facing fears, overcoming death,
   working through emotional distress
   and matters of ambition.

The Aspen Tree is aligned to the use of intuition and the uncovering or revelation of
secret or esoteric knowledge. Long have
Wizards sought Aspens as "Oracle Trees."

From a meditative state—the Body of Light —they watch as winds blowing through the leaves produce a sound and flickering sight that is conducive to skrying and receiving visions and prophecies. Slightly more robust, Poplar and Cottonwood Trees carry the same energy current. Cottonwood, particularly, is more highly aligned to masculine/solar polarities, also known as the "Giant Aspen."

The *Eadha* current represents mysterious lessons that are necessary to overcome in order for spiritual completion on the Earth Plane—and finally the "Grand Ascension." Aspen Trees have many associations with death, as both Jesus and Judas of the Judeo-Christian tradition hung from them. Aspen wands and *ward*-talismans represent overcoming death and bad habits. They are also used in "karmic balancing" rites and for revenge. The measuring rod used to fit coffins for people was once made of Aspen wood. But Aspen is not the final Ogham Tree in the twenty-fold system—it is nineteenth— reminding us that the physical death transition state is *not* the end.

Elves, Wizards and Druids all maintain a "Transmigration of Souls" doctrine that indicates that the "spiritual egg" at the center or core of our True Self is not physically tangible at the normal human degree of perception and is not destroyed when the physical body or vehicle perishes. It instead extends its own light to maintain a spiritual existence or vehicle fit for higher degrees/frequencies of manifestation. If more lessons must be learned, the Light Body or spiritual self will travel to another catalyst or vehicle to access this knowledge—we sometimes call *reincarnation*—which continues until a True Ascension takes place, and the being or spirit is so full of light that physical incarnations are no longer necessary, except in cases where a self-actualized Ascended Master returns by will to assist teaching others. The Aspen Tree does not have many medicinal uses, save one famous one: Nature's Aspirin. The bark is powdered and administered—perhaps in capsules or tea—to relieve fevers and mild tension or pain.

beech tree

Elvish-Celtic Names: Phagos, Sultan,
  Atarya Dwyrion, Ffawydden
Elvish-Ogham Letter: "Ph"
Druid Guardian: Pharon or Oberash
  (Alba-Sun)
Archetypes & Deities: The Sun, Virgil,
  Grandmother of the Forest, Ogmha
  (Ogma), Belinos, Lugh, Oenghus mac
  Og and Minerva.
Quadratic Element: Skyfire (or Water)
  Subordinate Element: Fire
Colour: Orange (or Sky Blue)
Polarity: Female (lunar) usually,
  otherwise reflective (crystalline).
Sacred Animal/Bird: *'Draig-Teine'* or
  FireDrake/Crane or Bluebird
Gemstones: Fire Opal, Blue Topaz,
  Azurite and Elf-Stones individually.
Ffayrie Herb(s): Morning Glory
Traditional Uses: Writing tablets,
  book covers, woodcraft, tree
  communication.
Divinatory & Energy Expressions:
  Archaic knowledge, writing (letters),
  communication (creativity),

Summer Solstice (*Alban Heruin*),
runes (learning), victory, and letting
go of old patterns.

Beech Trees are a secret Ogham character
incorporated into a later system—possibly
by reconstructionists themselves. It is an
important tree, appearing in the first line
of the "Cad Goddeu," yet it does not appear
in any traditional twenty-fold Ogham system. The Beech and Oak trees are the sub-
ject of the first quatrain of the "Cad Goddeu" prose—and they share a connection,
representing ultimate "Godparents of the
Forest" (*Atarya Dwyrion*). Elvish lore often
depicts the *Phagos* current as a more "feminine" counterpart of the "masculine" Oak.

Phagos is a sacred tree to both Elves and
Dragons. According to lore, Beech is more
closely aligned to humanoid energies than
other trees—and its "Dryad" spirit is often
more receptive to communication than
many other species. In spite of this, the
Beech Tree is often slighted out of "New
Age" texts regarding "trees in magic" that
are based exclusively on a modern 'Celtic
Tree Oracle' popularized by Liz and Colin

Murray. But there are other, and more anti-quated, resources regarding Ogham lore—much of which is found within the *Elve-nomicon* series volume titled: *"The Book of Ogham."* Communication is significant integral of the *Phagos* current. Beech wood was once the preferred material for writing tablets and even hardcover books. Resonating with the "preservation of knowledge," the *Phagos* current may also serve useful when working with ancestral spirits. The Beech Tree produces an edible nut called a *"mast,"* which is also traditionally used to make cooking oil.

birch tree

Elvish-Celtic Names: Beith, Beithe,
  Beth, Belwen, Bedwen
Ogham Letter: "B"
Druid Guardian: Boibel (Babel)
Archetypes & Deities: The Stars, New
  Moon, Bel, and the White Goddess.
Quadratic Element: Air
  Subordinate Element: Water
Colour: White (*'alban'* or *'ban'*)
Polarity: Female (lunar)

Month: November (New Year)
Sacred Animal/Bird: Cow/
   Pheasant (*'besan'*)
Gemstones: Flourite and the Silver
   Elf-Stone.
Ffayrie Herb(s): Fly Agaric Mushroom
Traditional Uses: Wands, broomsticks,
   protection for children and wards.
Divinatory & Energy Expressions:
   New beginnings, renewal, fertility,
   cleansing, purification and birth.

The Birch Tree marks the New Year on most interpretations of the Celtic Tree Calender and as such is sacred to *Samhain*. Its purifying energies are called to drive out old spirits and static energies of the old year. Such is also the primary ritual function of a "magical broom." Traditional folk magic rituals often began with sweeping out of the area to neutralizing the energy of a magical workspace or *Nemeton*. The "flying" aspect of the witchcraft tradition more likely emerged from the use of mushrooms that grew in the Birch shade and provoked "spirit flight" when ingested. Such methods of "astral travel" would lead seekers into the Otherworld via hallucinogens.[*]

Beith is an energy of new beginnings, and the tree is notorious for producing new trees from fallen twigs. As the first tree of the Ogham system, it is commonly the first forest lesson encountered by an initiate. Only as a result of effective abilities to awaken, communicate and utilize currents of the Birch Tree, would a first degree student of "Elementalism" be permitted to enter the second degree of "Forest Magick."

The New Year marks the annual transition into the "Dark Half of the Year"—from *Samhain* to *Beltane*. And although not observed even close *Samhain*, the Birch Tree is most closely aligned to energies of Spring Equinox (*Alban Eiler*) forcing many scholars to question the validity of the accepted "Tree Calender" used by reconstructionists.

The Birch Tree is the "Lady of the Woods"— often replacing the Beech as the Silver Pillar (next to the Ash/Yew and Oak) in the Forest Magickal Tradition. Medicinally, the oil from the bark may be used to make a

---

[*] For legal reasons we don't actually advocate this.

skin lotion, which may assist a variety of skin conditions. The buds of the Birch flowers are used to help stomach pains and ulcers. Chewing on twigs will helps keep teeth clean, and a tincture of the leaves and/or bark aids relieving mouth soars. Teas and tinctures have a purifying quality causing frequent urination when ingested. The oil in the bark may be used to repel insects. [Apparently, modern scientists discovered that a chemical in Birch known as "*methyl*," makes this all possible.]

blackthorne tree

Elvish-Celtic Names: Straif, Straife
Ogham Letters: "St" "Ss" and "Z"
Druid Guardian: Stru
Archetypes & Deities: Temperance
  (needed), The Falling Tower, The
  Arch Druid, Scathach and Skadi.
Quadratic Element: Earth
Colour: Purple or Bright ('*sorcha*')
Polarity: Female (lunar)
Other Trees Sharing the Current:
  Plum ('*emrys*')

Sacred Animal/Bird: Wolf and Black
   Cat/Thrush ('*stmolach*')
Gemstones: All Elf-Stones combined.
Ffayrie Herb(s): Stinging Nettle
Traditional Uses: 'Thunder and
   Lightning Staff' or 'Dark Staff' (a.k.a.
   '*shillelagh*'), cudgel weapons and
   warding against evil and illness.
Divinatory & Energy Expressions:
   Cleansing, control, use of force,
   confusion, restraint, blockages,
   resentment, strife, sudden change
   or renewal; and protective wards.

Blackthorne—also called "Wishing-thorne"
or the "Faerie Tree"—actively reflects the
"darker side" of Nature, and the thorns
may be carried (or used in ritual) as a symbol of this part of the "Ffayrie Tradition."
When allowed to grow wild, it forms an im-
penetrable bramble—yet it is important to
clarify that when allowed to grow, Blackthorne is a tree, not a bush.

In the physical "Green World," a hedge of
thorns may help to hide a grove or other
"secret portals" to the Otherworld. If we
apply the same symbolism to divination,

the hedge may represent barriers and distractions which promote confusion and anger.

Dark Power is not restricted to "Dark Elves" and actually has nothing to do with the *Unseelie Court*. Darkness and shadows simply hide those parts of the world—and ourselves—that we do not readily see or accept, like the "Shadow Self." When we see observe the manner in which we handle frustration and anger, we are often left to deal with aspects we do not like and may seek to change. You can't change the fact that sometimes you get thwarted on your path and will come across barriers and challenges. You can change your programmed fight-or-flight response-reactions and your ability to cope, or manage the "Game of Life."

A *"Shillelagh"* or *"Blasting Rod"* is made from a Blackthorne branch with Ogham signs of power burned along its surface. Lore suggests that a repetitive sequence of personal names and words of power would be inscribed thereon. In spite of its many titles, this is not a tool of malevolence. On the contrary, it was used to protect against such malignant energy in an active manner —perhaps as the original "ward-wand"—so as not to leave one defenseless against "Dark Arts." Strength, wisdom and self-actualization occur when you can face and control your own dark nature without being controlled by it. It cannot be healthily suppressed as "evil," because in doing so you are rejecting a part of yourself that will only surface later, unbidden and uncontrolled, and usually with unhealthy and/or destructive consequences.

Blackthorne tea—concocted from powdered bark—induces a calming effect, as is a common aspect of many Ffayrie trees when ingested, which may help to slow one's vibration to "Green World" frequencies. Blackthorne produces a purple berry called a "*sloe*," which is a necessary ingredient for "sloe-gin" alcohol. Ink and dye are also made from the sloe berry. It is most sacred to *Samhain*, and second to *Beltane*.

cedar tree

Elvish-Celtic Name: Chakris
Elvish-Ogham Letter: "Ch"
Druid Guardian: Shavae
Archetypes & Deities: The Sacred
    Grove, Brighid, Arianrhod and
    Wotan.
Quadratic Element: Air
Colour: Blue, Green or Pale Yellow.
Polarity: Masculine (solar)
Sacred Animal/Bird: Ewe/Goldfinch
Gemstones: Yellow Chrysopraise and
    the Gold Elf-Stone.
Ffayrie Herb(s): Juniper
Traditional Uses: Purification, space
    clearing and home blessings; also
    calling and summoning spirits.
Divinatory & Energy Expressions:
    Clearing out the old to make way for
    heights of psychic (spiritual) aware-
    ness, spiritual abilities and the
    knowledge of one's own spiritual
    timeline (past incarnations, &tc).

Cedar is not a traditional Ogham tree. Along
with the Beech, it was incorporated into the
system more recently. The wood carries a

long-standing tradition in the Ancient Near East for "binding" spiritual energies, and is traditionally used in construction of many sacred buildings such as Solomon's Temple.

Some "New Age" Ogham revival systems classify the *Chakris* rune as the "the Grove" (*"Koad"*), most likely named after the Ceder Tree's ability to purify the area of the Grove (*Nemeton*). The runic glyph and energy current, however, is more appropriately attributed to the Cedar as an individual tree. In Elven Forest Magick, Cedar wood (and essence) is a purification incense, used in a similar manner as "sage." The smoke may be assist consecrating the Circle of Power, especially if ritual intentions include spirit summoning, ancestral work, or any form of Mesopotamian Neopaganism. It is called the "Tree of Light," sacred to the *Imbolc* and, as an evergreen, to the winter season (*Alban Arthuan*) and "Yule."

cherry tree

Elvish-Celtic Name: Oadha
Elvish Letters: "Da" "Dh" and "Th"
Druid Guardian: Ambash

Archetypes & Deities: The Wild Hunt, Herne and Pan

Quadratic Element: Fire

Colour: Burnt-umber

Polarity: Masculine (solar)

Sacred Animal/Bird: Bear/Red-Tailed Hawk and the Phoenix.

Gemstones: Obsidian, Sard(onyx), and Crystalline Elf-Stone.

Ffayrie Herb(s): Cherry Fruit and Flowers

Traditional Uses: Communication with animals (brown magick,) kindling sacred fires only, declaring and ending wars, woodcarving.

Divinatory & Energy Expressions: Sweetness, joy, delight, passion, love, conflict, competition and attraction (desire), healing (after conflict or loss)

Cherry is a popular wood for art and wood-craft because of its distinct coloration and ease of workability. The wood is naturally charged to amplify Will, alchemy or trans-formation magick. The current can be used for intentions that further an existing war, or to end and prevent them.

Cherries are symbolic of sexual passion—the power and intensity of the orgasm, and is sacred to *Beltane* and Midsummer (or *Alban Heruin*). *Oadha* is not an official Ogham Tree and yet, it seems incomplete not to consider it in our catalogue.

elder tree

Elvish-Celtic Names: Ruis, Ysgawen
Ogham Letter: "R"
Druid Guardian: Ruben
Archetypes & Deities: The "Hanged Man," Vulcan, Boann and Nikneven.
Quadratic Element: Earth
Colour: Blood Red (*'ruadh'*)
Polarity: Crystalline or Female (lunar)
Month: The 13th Month (*Samhain*)
Other Trees Sharing the Current: Bourtree
Sacred Animal/Bird: Badger and Black Sow/Pheasant or Rook (*'rocknat'*).
Gemstones: Bloodstone, Red Jasper and the Crystalline Elf-Stone.
Ffayrie Herb(s): Nightshades
Traditional Uses: Exorcism, banishing, regeneration magick, elderberry

wine and faerie-sight ointment.
Divinatory & Energy Expressions:
   Self-reflection (examination), the
   end of a cycle (regeneration),
   completion, change and crossroads.
* NOT TO BE CUT FOR WOOD!
* LEAVES MAY BE POISONOUS!

Some superstitious folklore mistakenly attributes Elder as an "unlucky tree," but Elven-Faerie lore simply says that it is unlucky to cut one down, bring inside or even grow indoors. Those who cut them might fall to misfortune and death—and thus you have been warned now of this Forest Code. Elder Knowledge is "Crone Knowledge," demanding protection and preservation—just as the elders of a spiritual society and their folk memory require the same. For *Ogham-ancers*, the *Ruis* current is one of the most difficult to awaken for "Tree Communication."

Elder is not a particularly large tree, reaching only 30 feet in height at maturity—but it is powerful and resilient. Its wood is strong, withstanding many harsh conditions. Elder bark—found as deadwood—may be used to develop a very dark dye and the leaves yield a rich "forest green" hue often used for riding/traveling cloaks. When mixed with alum and salt, the wood produces a deep violet dye. The Elder Tree is very sacred in Elven-Ffayrie traditions, even apart from its Oghamic associations. According to lore, its sap may be used as to make a "Faerie-Sight" ointment—a headdress or diadem fashioned from Elder deadwood twigs may grant the same ability to its wearer.

As previously stated, Elder is the "Crone of the Forest," the "Venerable Mother." She is so sacred to the forest people that her wood is protected in Celtic society by a *"geis,"* a taboo against removing livewood—even by Wizards. Those who use the wood for furniture and miscellany may be haunted by the spirits of the wood, and fall upon misfortune. [DeLorean cleared an ancient Elder and Thorn Faerie-forest to make room for a new car manufacturing plant in Ireland, and the company practically disappeared.]

"Dark-natured" trees, called "unlucky" by some, actually tend to be the best species/

types for ridding a space of negative energy or clearing away illness. Folklore suggests a tincture of "Elder Flow'r" will purify the bloodstream. Leaves may be infused into a solution that for externally dressing bruises and swellings—or as a pesticide. Elderberries are rich in Vitamin C and are used to make a delicious wine. They may also be boiled down to make a shampoo that will have a darkening effect on the hair.

the fir-pine-elm current

Elvish-Celtic Names: Ailim, Ailm, Elma, Ffynidwydden, Pinwydden

Ogham Letter: "A"

Druid Guardian: Achab

Archetypes & Deities: Green Man or Horned One, Merlyn, Abban, Gaea (Am-Mesh), Arianrhod, Mithra and Sezh

Quadratic Element: Earth
Subordinate Element: Fire

Colour: Jade Green, Light Blue or Speckled (*'alad'*)

Polarity: Masculine (solar), but also aligned to the Earth Mother.

Other Trees Sharing the Current:
Redwood

Sacred Animal/Bird: Cow, Stag or
Deer/Lapwing (*'aidhirdeog'*)

Gemstones: Moss Agate and all three
Elf-Stones combined or as individual
currents.

Ffayrie Herb(s): Cowslip

Traditional Uses: Forest Magick,
regeneration magick, Earth-wands,
torches and for sacred fires.

Divinatory & Energy Expressions:
The Elves, ancient knowledge,
primal power, high views or
objectivity, penetration, strength
and the eternal Earth-memory.

Fir/Pine/Elm trees represent pure primal
Earth elemental and planetary energetic
currents and an interconnectivity with all
life in the Green World of Nature—which is
the epitome of the "Green Ray."

The Elm is especially distinguished as the
"Tree of Elves," and carries the same *geas*
taboo against its use as the Elder. As a result of the now frequent Dutch-Elm Disease,
the species is not often planted/cultivated

in modern society. Overcoming this barrier of disease reflects the true strength inherent in the *Elma* part of the current—and certainly the Elm shares many spiritual attributes with the Fir/Pine (*Ailm*) part of this energy, carrying affinities for "invisbility magick," agriculture and protective rites.

Fir and Pine Trees are tall and slender in comparison to the Elm. They are also evergreens—the Elm is deciduous. The tallness of the Fir, Pine and Redwood varieties demonstrate their "objectivity" and "high view"—their ability to see clearly and judge fairly. They are also quite communicative. They are able to grow new trees from old sprouts thought to be dead, making the Fir-Pine an iconic symbol of endurance, eternal life, and of course, regeneration—which is why it is popularly featured in winter.

We can use modern science to divide this current into hundreds of sub-species, but all of them represent the "Middle Pillar" and carry the energy of the "Green Ray" in its clearest form. Ease of communicating with this current and its frequent appearance in Sylvan Magick makes it a prime candidate for early novice "tree work" before approaching other primer trees in the forest catalogue, such as Birch and Beech. The *Ailim* current is useful for growth and fertility rites—for both the "Green World" and personal needs, as well as rituals and ceremonies pertaining to marriage and relationships. Pine is also a natural source of charcoal, tar and turpentine.

furze and gorse

Elvish-Celtic Names: Ohn, Piswydden
Ogham Letter: "O"
Druid Guardian: Oise
Archetypes & Deities: The Sun, Lugh
    and Adraste.
Quadratic Element: Fire
    Subordinate Element: Air
Colour: Yellow and Gold (*'odhar'*)
Polarity: Masculine (solar)
Other Trees Sharing the Current:
    Spindle (*'gwyrthed'*), the Linden Tree
    (*'ohun'*) and Basswood or Lime tree.
Sacred Animal/Bird: Rabbits and
    Bees/Scrat (*'odoroscrach'*)
Gemstones: Peridot and Gold ElfStone.

Ffayrie Herb(s): Heather
Traditional Uses: Honey, food for
   animals, fertility magick and
   purification.
Divinatory & Energy Expressions:
   Wisdom, spiritual fulfillment,
   optimism, projection (like rays) and
   protection.

To call this Ogham a "tree" is bit of a stretch, but this hedge plant does grow a woody "bark" and it appears in the "*Cad Goddeu*" prose, describing a "Battle of the Trees." Some scholars believe the "Battle of the Trees" was a metaphysical skirmish to determine rank and stature of the species composing the later Druidic Ogham Tradition. This low prickly shrub—not typically taller than a Human—is often present for purification rites and/or burned as incense.

To work with this current directly in your locale, you may need to find a suitable substitute tree that shares its energy—such as a *Linden* or *Lime* tree—especially if you intend to construct an *Ohn*-wand. The Gorse-Furze Ogham is also closely related to "Broom" and "*Ohun*," the Linden Tree or

Basswood—but Americans without access to a Gorse bush are probably not going to find a species of Linden Tree naturally growing nearby either. "*Ohun*" is sacred to stars and astronomy, but also to magical rites or enchantments regarding love, beauty, glamour and personal attraction. Its metaphysical/"*ray*" color is orange—as opposed to yellow for Gorse—but it retains a strong alignment with the element of Fire.

hawthorn tree

Elvish-Celtic Names: Huatha, Huath, Draenen Wen
Ogham Letter: "H"
Druid Guardian: Huiria
Archetypes & Deities: Judgment, Balance, Olwen and Hurle
Quadratic Element: Fire
  Subordinate Element: Air
Colour: Purple or "Terrible" ('*huath*')
Polarity: Crystalline
Month: April
Sacred Animal/Bird: Dragon or Goat/Night Raven ('*aadaig*')
Gemstones: Amethyst, Tanzanite and

any related Elf-Stones.

Ffayrie Herb(s): Primrose Flow'r and
May Blossoms.

Traditional Uses: Love and marriage
rites, wands and wards acquired
between April 21 or Beltane (May
1st) and the end of May. The wood is
not usually taken otherwise or is
grown live for magickal protection.

Divinatory & Energy Expressions:
Purity, restraint, chastity (but also
love and marriage) and prosperity.

Hawthorn is a "Faerie tree" with a special
"*geis*" (*taboo*) against wood removal—except
during a ten-day period preceding *Beltane*
when wizardwood may be properly ob-
tained in keeping with tradition. *Huatha*
staves, wards and wands all have powerful
protective properties, particularly against
enchantment, spells or magic from others.
This wood is also used to make the famous
"Whitewand," just as Blackthorne wood is
used to make the "Darkstaff." As with any
cutting, a ceremonial rite should accom-
pany wizardwood removal as a sign of re-
spect toward the spirits residing within
that otherwise may bring misfortune.

Often cut back to form a "haw" or hedge, the hawthorn may enjoy a long time—even by tree standards—and reach dozens of feet in height. It makes a frequent appearance in fantasy or "fairy tales" as a magical barrier or wall around enchanted places or castles. Some Elven lore refers to it as the "Wishing Tree." Hawthorn berries, raw or in tea, may act as a blood thinner with calming properties to assist relieving heart issues. If the oak-resembling leaves are added to the tea, it may help a sore throat—and is sometimes added to grain alcohol for the same result.

hazel tree

Elvish-Celtic Names: Coll, Koll, Collen
Ogham Letters: "C" and "K"
Druid Guardian: Kay (*'Cai'*)
Archetypes & Deities: High Priestess,
   Star Mother (Goddess,) Llyr and
   Mannan mac Llyr.
Quadratic Element: Water
   Subordinate Element: Air
Colour: Midnight Blue, Brown (*'cron'*)
Polarity: Feminine (lunar)

Month: July
Sacred Animal/Bird: Salmon/Crane
Gemstones: Lapis Lazuli, Sapphire and
    the Silver Elf-Stone.
Ffayrie Herb(s): Bullrush
Traditional Uses: 'Dowsing Rods,'
    wands, divination sticks, baskets
    and thatch work. The nuts are used
    for love spells and to make drinks to
    induce 'Spirit Vision'; Beltane.
Divinatory & Energy Expressions:
    Manifesting creativity, divination,
    intuition (understanding), spirit
    vision and skrying.

The Hazel Tree provides an energetic current of great insight. Its nuts fall into lakes,
which feed the "Salmon of Wisdom." The
stream of Hazel-Salmon energy is the current or path of "inner knowledge," what is
often sought from oracles and in divination:
"perfect cosmic knowledge of all things."
Hazel rods may be used to form an entire
set of divination sticks—when tied together
or carried in a "Crane bag" or pouch, actually represent a powerful ancient protective
amulet. Forked branches are sometimes
used to make "dowsing rods"—tools of en-

ergy-testing, for finding water, or tracking "ley lines."

Elven lore suggests that the energetic current of the "Hazelnut Tree" represents the "Tree of Sacred Knowledge"—a catalyst for learning the true nature of the *Self* and the Universe, and should not be confused with Eden's "Tree of Knowledge," which is metaphoric—or ancient near eastern allegory—and related to genetics.

The nuts of the Hazel tree are edible, and may be powdered to infuse a drink to induce "spirit vision," as well aid relieving colds and sore throat symptoms. The Water element is strong in Hazel energy, especially when found growing around water. Its energy is most similar to that of the Willow Tree and *Saille* Ogham current.

heather and mistletoe

Elvish-Celtic Names: Ur (Heather), Uchelwydd (Mistletoe)
Ogham Letters: "U" and "W"
Druid Guardian: Uriath
Archetypes & Deities: The Hermit, All

Heal, Freya and Grainne
Quadratic Element: Air
Colour: Purple or "Resinous" (*'usgdha'*)
Polarity: Crystalline
Sacred Animal/Bird: Bee and Lion/
   Lark (*'uiseog'*)
Gemstones: The Three Elf-Stones.
Ffayrie Herb(s): Heather and
   Honeysuckle.
Traditional Uses: Healing (mistletoe);
   attracting rain, perfume (Heather)
Divinatory & Energy Expressions:
   Healing, clarity, reviving, All-Heal
   (mistletoe) and passion.

There are two types of *Ur*-Heather: red and white. The Red type attracts passion and is a symbol of sexual energy and lust. White Heather wards against passion and sex and symbolizes purity and chastity. While Red Heather is sacred to, and picked, at Midsummer (or *Alban Huruin*), White Heather is aligned to Spring Equinox (or *Alban Eiler*). Heather is not a tree, but is listed as one of the Ogham energetic currents, and is therefore listed here.

In some versions of the system, this Ogham sign and energetic current is actually represented by "Mistletoe," which Elven and Drwyd lore both suggest is among the most sacred of all herbs. Naturally, both Heather and the Mistletoe current share similar attributes.

Mistletoe lore is mainly the product of Celtic Druid Tradition. It was considered most powerful when found growing on Oak Trees —a rare but very real event (in spite of what modern skeptics have to say on it). Mistletoe is aligned with the Air Element because it passes itself along tree top canopies. It is a 'parasitic plant' that attaches to a host tree and does not root in the ground itself. When cut with the Druid's Sickle, a white linen sheet would be placed below to catch it, being sure that its sacred essence never touched the ground. This herb was then consecrated and later added to all Druidic medicines—lending Mistletoe the folklore name "All Heal."

holly tree

Elvish-Celtic Names: Tinne, Celynen

Ogham Letter: "T"

Druid Guardian: Teilmon

Archetypes & Deities: The Golden Chariot, the Holly Man/King, Arawn, Govannan, Hades, Ares and Persephone.

Quadratic Element: Fire

Colour: Dark Gray ('*temen*')

Polarity: Solar (masculine)

Month: June

Sacred Animal/Bird: Warhorse and Warhound/Starling ('*truith*')

Gemstones: Ruby and Gold Elf-Stone.

Ffayrie Herb(s): Monk's Hood (Aconite)

Traditional Uses: Spear making (combat and protection), Midwinter/ Yule, chariot wheels, charcoal and grown live to bring good fortune and ward off evil.

Divinatory & Energy Expressions: Movement, vigor, "Best in Fight" (courage and success), sacredness (holiness), the Wheel of the Year

(*Cor Anar*), and Nature's cycles.

Many modern Christmas customs are derived from ancient Elven-Faerie Druidism ('*Drwyddon*')—the ancient national religion of Celtic people once dominating the British Isles, Ireland, and previously, the European mainland. Holly is actually an evergreen bush, but it may have served as the first traditional "Yuletide Tree." Of course, all evergreens share some affinity with winter. Holly berries also hang like red ball-ornaments, inspiring iconic color themes for its seasonal festivals. The three primary Druidic herbs significant to Yule actually represent three 'Oghams' directly—Holly, Ivy and Mistletoe.

Lore suggests to grow a Holly Tree in your grove or garden to attract positive currents and ward against negative energy. Hollywood burns well when still green (freshly cut) but it is taboo and against the Faerie Code to do so. Burning any pre-dried wood, particularly a species held so sacred to Elven-Ffayrie, is blasphemous. Holly wands may summon lightning, suggesting fire alignment as is the relationship with war and allegorical conflict of ongoing struggle for annual supremacy between the Oak King, ruler of the "light half of the year" and the Holly King who is keeper of the "dark half of the year."

The *Tinne* current shares many of the same energetic attributes as the Oak Tree—and with good reason. The only major frequency difference (aside from obvious size) is that Holly is an evergreen and Oak is not. At Midsummer (*Alban Heruin*) the Oak King loses the battle over the Sun's control to the Holly King, who yields it back to the Oak King on *Holly Day*, or approximately Yule. This is metaphorical, of course, and the lore is used to describe or explain the properties and polarity of natural forces that ebb and flow at varying times of year. [Holly leaves may also be used to brew detoxifying teas.]

the ivy

Elvish-Celtic Names: Gort, Uruin, Eiddew
Ogham Letter: "G"
Druid Guardian: Gahth

Archetypes & Deities: Justice, the
Golden Spiral, the Swan Maidens,
Cuchulain, Cernunnos/Kerununnos
and Orion.

Quadratic Element: Earth

Colour: Sky Blue (*'gorm'*)

Polarity: Feminine (lunar)

Month: September

Sacred Animal/Bird: Boar/
Swan (*'geis'*)

Gemstones: Chrysoberyl and related
Elf-Stones.

Ffayrie Herb(s): Lichen and Moss.

Traditional Uses: Exorcism rites and
used to make the spiral that wraps
around natural wands.

Divinatory & Energy Expressions:
Cooperation, healing and the 'inner
spiral' (journey of the 'spirit').

In the helix-style growth pattern of the Ivy,
ancient Elves and Druids observed and recorded the "Golden Spiral"—else, the energetic serpent-entwining of DNA structures
and life patterns. While not generally clas-
sified as a tree, Ivy possesses an ability to
develop bark and grow strong when allowed to. *Gort* unifies the spiral with the

wand—as a spiral (carved or metal) is some-times wrapped around the length of a wand —or for a true herbalist, this might be the Ivy itself. Spirals represent active creation, so incorporating it with any magical tool (or object) provides an additional "active" quality. It is sacred to the Autumn Equinox (or *Alban Elved*).

maple tree

Elvish-Celtic Name: Shorin
Ogham Letter: "Sh"
Druid Guardian: Mabon
Archetypes & Deities: Ymir (Norse)
   and Mabon son of Modron (Celtic)
Quadratic Element: Fire
   Subordinate Element: Earth
Colour: Fiery Red, Orange or Amber
Polarity: Masculine (solar)
Sacred Animal/Bird: Fox/Horned Owl
Gemstones: Gold Elf-Stone, especially
   the Tiger's Eye.
Traditional Uses: Spells of binding,
   strength and unity of family, maple
   syrup; red and orange-ray magick;
   the Autumn Equinox (*Alban Elved*).

Divinatory & Energy Expressions:
Energy (vibrancy), strength, good
fortune, transformation, family life.

The Maple Tree is not a traditional Ogham character. In fact, it is not mentioned anywhere in "Celtic" Ogham lore. Maple is included here because North American and Canadian practitioners *do* share access to this energetic current, and it is a powerful one—quite common to encounter in these geographic locales.

The Celtic Tree Ogham was refined by Ancient Druids of Ireland, a location where the *Shorin* current has little lore is ascribed to it. Its leaf structure is iconic—even gracing the Canadian national flag—visibly displaying the 'Sign of Elves' and 'Rays'. The leaves transition through all hues of green-to-red in Autumn, near "Equinox" (or *Alban Elved*). Maples may be used for magic to connect with similar energies—tree types or species that are not accessible to where the practitioner resides. Wands are appropriate for sex magick—in its purest sense: awakening inspiration or creativity and then manifesting it.

oak tree

Elvish-Celtic Names: Duir, Dwyr, Dar, Derwen

Ogham Letter: "D"

Druid Guardian: Daivaith or Dagda

Archetypes & Deities: The Emperor, the Oak King, the 'Flaming Door,' Obraash, Lugh, Dagda, W'Odin, Hu, Thor and Helios (the Sun).

Quadratic Element: Fire

Colour: Gold and Black (*'dub'*)

Polarity: Masculine (solar)

Other Trees Sharing the Current: Hickory, Pecan.

Month: May

Other Trees Sharing the Current: Hickory (see also *Holly Tree*)

Sacred Animal/Bird: White Mare, Lion (Tiger), Salamander, Serpent or Adder/Peacock or Wren (*'druin'*)

Gemstones: Yellow Topaz, Amber (petrified tree sap), Gold and the Gold Elf-Stone.

Ffayrie Herb(s): Acorn (*'uri'* or *'uru'*) and Mistletoe.

Traditional Uses: Protection for homes

and doors, Elven-Druid magick,
fertility magick, timber (especially
for doors, bats, sticks and clubs).
The 'gall' can be used as a powerful
talisman called *"Naddred"* —the
"Adder's Egg" "Druid's Egg" or
"Druid's Gem."

Divinatory & Energy Expressions:
Strength, leadership, material gain,
longevity (endurance), opening the
doorway (to the mysteries), ineffable
(solid) truth and solid protection.

Oak-acorns are fiery seeds of life—perhaps
one of the most famous elf-amulets found
in Nature and used to attract fertility, love
and protection. Oak Groves—collectives of
trees—have a tendency to grow because, as
is said, the "acorn never falls far from the
tree." Elven and Druid lore suggests that
eating the acorns—or using oak flour—may
aid in understanding "Divine" (Cosmic) and
ineffable truth via inspiration (or *'gnosis'*),
as similar to the *Hazelnut*. The Oak is a very
"busy" tree with vast long-standing traditions of mystic lore—and it may very well
be the most sacred tree on Earth.

Deep within the Greenwood forest stands a tall and gnarled Oak Tree branching out wide and drawing you nearer and nearer to the mysteries of the secret grove—the repository for all knowledge in Nature. There lies the "great door" leading to the inner mysteries of true initiation. True magick is what brings us "Absolute Truth" and contributes to our evolution on the "Path of Ascension."

Oak is often used to represent highest degrees or levels of study in Elvish Schools of Druidism, emphasizing a path to self-realization and absolute awareness. It embodies the final most notable lesson for Oghamancers in their advancement to the "*Drywydd*" degree and is listed seventh in the Ogham alphabet, perhaps demonstrating a hidden awareness and appreciation of the original and complete "sevenfold" system.

There is an old saying about how Oak is a long-lived tree: "300 years to grow, 300 years to mature, 300 years to die." In that time they will commonly acquire what are known as "galls." These spherical growths are sometimes the result of insect hives occupying beneath the trunk surface until their larvae are mature.

The "Grandfather of the Forest," guards the Oak door of May at *Beltane* and clearly aligned to the Fire Element. In fact, the *Duir* tree current carries such an affinity with fire that it has a tendency to manifest the element as lightning—which seems to strike Oaks more than any other species observed, almost as if they are "calling it down." Obviously the species defends its attributes of "strength and endurance" by withstanding such energy, resulting often in a more gnarled, tangled and "interesting" looking tree. The fiery energetic affinity between Duir and lightning makes a Golden Oak-wand (a companion to the Silver Apple-wand) highly prized for powerful Nature-oriented magic.

Oak wood is a common material for ceremonial blade handles (corresponding with its fire alignment)—and another tree that closely shares the *Duir* energy current, though perhaps more passively, is the Hickory Tree or "*axara*." Its energetic attributes are similar to Oak, but applying to more worldly, mundane or tangible aspects—such as the acquisition of material gain, good fortune and abundance. In fact, oak-hickory forests are among the most common in North America east of the Mississippi River.

reed and broom

Elvish-Celtic Names: Ngetal, Corsen, Erun

Ogham Letter: "Ng"

Druid Guardian: Noimahr

Archetypes & Deities: The Wheel of Fortune, Olbaal, Gwydion, Morgana and Morrighan.

Quadratic Element: Air
   Subordinate Element: Water

Colour: Grass Green (*'nglas'*)

Polarity: Feminine (lunar)

Month: October

Sacred Animal/Bird: Dog and Stag/Goose (*'ngeigh'*)

Gemstones: Aquamarine and the appropriate Elf-Stones.

Ffayrie Herb(s): Reed and Broom

Traditional Uses: Fertility, Love Magick, writing pens, brooms and

pipes.
Divinatory & Energy Expressions:
Effort, direct action, application and
harmony.

Broom is a specific kind of tall wetland
grass known as reed. It literally grows out
of the water—and may even form an outer
bark layer—making it the "Water Tree" of
Elven Forest Tradition, though other systems often reserve this title for the Willow
tree. But, while Reed is derived from the
water, it is aligned with the Air element
with a long-standing affinity for communication, writing and knowledge that origin-
ates in the *Ancient Near East*, specifically
Babylon—where use of the "Reed stylus" was
perfected for refined cuneiform script.

Reed represents a connection between the
perceived "inner" and "outer" worlds and
the harmonic balance of those energies.
The Ngetal Ogham current is a subtle energy, slowly working its magic and enchantment from a point of stillness, with
small ripples. Although aligned to air, the
natural affinity between Reed/Broom and
water makes it an appropriate addition to

any rites aligned to an "aquatic" nature, or the consecration of water-elemental tools. The Broom type is actually named for its use in broom manufacture. In a previous lesson-chapter we discussed how brooms were used to sweep out and clear ritual space. Ironically, the Broom—both in its plant form or as an object—is sacred to *Samhain*.

rowen tree

Elvish-Celtic Names: Luis, Ceridinen
Ogham Letter: "L"
Druid Guardian: Loth
Archetypes & Deities: The Star, Epona
    and Macha.
Quadratic Element: Air
    Subordinate Element: Earth & Fire
Colour: Red or Gray (*'liath'*)
Polarity: Feminine (lunar)
Month: November
Other Names for this Current:
    Mountain Ash, "Quickening Tree"
Sacred Animal/Bird: Bear, Unicorn/
    Duck (*'lachu'*)
Gemstones: Smokey Quartz, Diamond,

Silver and appropriate Elf-Stones.
Ffayrie Herb(s): Yarrow
Traditional Uses: Empowerment,
   protection against enchantment,
   astral bridges (the 'spirit-world' and
   'Otherworld').
Divinatory & Energy Expressions:
   Awareness, insight, empowerment,
   self-control, evanescence,
   protection and nurturance.

The Rowen (also spelled 'Rowan') Tree produces berries, which, much like fruit from the Apple Tree, contains a five-pointed pentagram, traditionally symbolic of Nature's Elemental forces. These edible berries are rich in Vitamin A and C.

Talismans of Rowen wood offer protection while traveling and from the enchantments of others. For this reason, it is commonly used for walking sticks or staves and its protective properties make it beneficial to plant a Rowen Tree at the entrance of your home, property and/or Sacred Grove. *Luis* is called the "Quickening Tree" because of its active magickal power—combining active Air Elemental qualities with the feminine current. This Air of Moon correspondence makes its wizardwood a prime choice for a traditional "witches wand."

The flowers and berries often bear a pentagram and along with the leaves, once dried, may be used as incense. Don't forget to add a pinch of Mistletoe. Burning this may call forth energies of the ancestral realm and Otherworld—as well as the "Nature Spirits."

The Rowen is represented by the Unicorn, the epitome of all that is beautiful and enchanting, also representing a link between worlds. The Unicorn current tempers that of the Dragon. These energies should always be used in balance of one another. It is easy to fall into the trap of over-analyzing and over-thinking and essentially all of the untempered qualities of the unbalanced "Dragonmind." It is most sacred to the annual beginning of winter (*Samhain*).

the vine

Elvish-Celtic Names: Muin,
    Gwynwydden
Ogham Letter: "M"

Druid Guardian: Muriath
Archetypes & Deities: "The Lovers."
Quadratic Element: Water
Colour: Variegated (*'mbracht'*)
Polarity: Feminine (lunar)
Month: August
Sacred Animal/Bird: Scorpion and
   Lizard/Titmouse (*'mintan'*)
Gemstones: Aquamarine and the
   appropriate Elf-Stones.
Ffayrie Herb(s): Neckweede/marijuana
   and Blackberry/Raspberry.
Traditional Uses: Grapes, wine,
   meditation and revealing truths.
Divinatory & Energy Expressions:
   Inner-development, growth,
   self-realization and comprehension.

The Vine, though not necessarily a tree, is ranked among the Ogham currents because it may develop a hardened outer bark. Its sacred annual threshold time is the harvest, specifically the Autumn Equinox (or *Alban Elved*). It has been used to make grape-wine for thousands of years. A tradition of wine used to "reveal truths" is derived from its ability to gain information gathered via loss of inhibitions. *Muin* represents hidden, just-below-the-surface realizations—sometimes only brought to the surface when dis-inhib-ited—that cannot be healthily suppressed if we are to break through to the next steps of our progression. With an ability to scale walls, the Vine truly knows no boundaries.

willow tree

Elvish-Celtic Names: Saille, Awn, Helyg, Helygen
Ogham Letter: "S"
Druid Guardian: Saliath
Archetypes & Deities: The Moon, The Silver Huntress, Diana of the Forest, Arianrhod, Artemis, and Selene.
Quadratic Element: Water
Colour: Bright, Opalescent or "Fine" ('*sodath*')
Polarity: Feminine (lunar)
Month: February
Sacred Animal/Bird: Hare and Cat/Owl and Hawk ('*seg*')
Gemstones: Opal, Pearl and the Silver Elf-Stone.
Ffayrie Herb(s): Moonwort
Traditional Uses: Lunar magick,

feminine magick, fertility magick,
banishing depression, baskets and
wicker-work; dowsing rods and
divination; salicylic acid.
Divinatory & Energy Expressions:
Beauty, enchantment, rhythms,
cycles, secrets, and an indication
emotional healing is necessary.

Willow Trees possess a high affinity for water: it drinks a lot of it, soaking up as much
as possible to develop a fast growing trunk
structure. A combination of water and the
moon "*Rays*" contribute energetic qualities
of intuition, emotion, beauty and enchantment. Willow represents the epitome of the
lunar-water current resonating with the
"Moon Goddess" or "Triple Moon Goddess,"
aligned to feminine rhythms and cycles,
and not only regarding monthly rhythms,
but the greater life-cycle phases of "maid-
en-mother-crone."

The Willow is metaphorically the "Grandmother of the Forest"—the one you can tell
anything to because she has already been
there herself. A Willow-wand may be used
for lunar rites and/or water-oriented mag-

ick relating to feminine needs, as well as dreams and the old priestess tradition of "drawing down the moon." Its wood is also favored for fashioning 'dowsing rods'.

Saille is a healing Ogham, mostly on an emotional level. By linking/communing personally with Willows, you may open channels necessary to sort, retain and release past emotional pains and carried energy. Willow bark is also known for its healing properties, yielding the *salicylic acid* used in both aspirin and skin-acne treatments.

yew tree

Elvish-Celtic Names: Ioho, Ywen
Ogham Letters: "I" "J" and "Y"
Druid Guardian: Iachim
Archetypes & Deities: "Death," Arawn,
  Arianrhod, Maeve, the Dagda Mor
  and Hermes.
Quadratic Element: Earth
  Subordinate Element: Air
Colour: Dark Green or Very White
  (*'irfind'*)
Polarity: Crystalline

Sacred Animal/Bird: Spider/
    Eagle or Eaglet (*'illait'*)
Gemstones: Emerald and the Three
    Elf-Stones.
Ffayrie Herb(s): Bryony
Traditional Uses: Bows, poison and
    poisoned weapons.
Divinatory & Energy Expressions:
    Completion, changes, renewal,
    transformation forthcoming rebirth,
    the next step, the life and death
    cycle and communication.
* BERRIES MAY BE POISONOUS!

An evergreen marking the end of our magical forest journey, the Yew Tree reminds us that it cannot be a true ending—because nothing ends. By riding this energetic current toward Ascension, we are reborn and transformed into a new life. After completing the "Initiation of the Forest," the Initiate or "Oghamancer" may rightfully call themselves a "Sylvan Wizard" with the ability to awaken the woods and be known to all "Nature-spirits" as a forest-friend or "elf-friend."

Yew also stands at the finale of the Ogham alphabet. *Ioho* is the Oghamic sign of completion, in a manner much deeper than that represented by the *Ruis*-Elder Tree current. It is not so much an "ending," as much as it represents the gateway to the Otherworld—or that is to say the absolute promise that there is continuation of spiritual life after material death. *Ioho*-Yew shares an energetic frequency with a select few other Ogham Trees in the tendency to (re)generate new trees from its "*layrs.*"

The journey most certainly does not stop here. Mastery requires more than a few hours book-reading and a handful of visits into the forest. A perfection of the arts presented within the volumes of the *Elvenomicon* series will require many years of true and faithful dedication, observation, personal reflection, extensive practice and holistic immersion...

...into Secret Traditions of the
Druids, Elves and Faerie!

Would

you

like

to

know

more

???

CLASSICS OF MARDUKITE MESOPOTAMIA
REVISED HARDCOVER 2-VOLUME SET

SUMERIAN RELIGION

Introducing the Anunnaki Gods
of Mesopotamian Neopaganism

Mardukite Liber-50

by Joshua Free

BABYLONIAN MYTH & MAGIC

Spiritual Traditions and Mysticism
in Mesopotamian Anunnaki Religion

Mardukite Liber-51+E

by Joshua Free

SYSTEMOLOGY BASICS HARDCOVER SET

THE POWER OF ZU

Applying Mardukite Zuism and
Systemology to Everyday Life
Systemology Liber-S1-Z
based on a lecture series
by Joshua Free

THE WAY INTO THE FUTURE

A Handbook for the New Human
Systemology Liber-S1-W
collected works mini-anthology
by Joshua Free

SYSTEMOLOGY
The Pathway to Self-Honesty

GO FURTHER AND BE

CRYSTAL CLEAR

JOSHUA FREE

CRYSTAL CLEAR

(Handbook for Seekers)

Mardukite Systemology Liber-2B
by Joshua Free

Take control of your destiny
and chart the first steps
toward your own spiritual evolution.
Realize new potentials of the
Human Condition with
a Self-guiding handbook for
Self-Processing toward
Self-Actualization
in Self-Honesty using actual
techniques and training
provided for the coveted
"Mardukite Systemology Grade-III
Self-Defragmentation Course Program"
—once only available
directly and privately from
the underground Systemology Society.

Discover the amazing power behind the
applied spiritual technology
used for counseling and advisement in
the tradition of Mardukite Zuism.

19 95   20 20

JOSHUA FREE

PUBLISHED BY THE **JOSHUA FREE** IMPRINT REPRESENTING

The Mardukite Academy of Systemology

THE JOSHUA FREE IMPRINT
JFI PUBLICATIONS

MARDUKITE
ZUISM

mardukite.com

www.ingramcontent.com/pod-product-compliance
Lightning Source LLC
Chambersburg PA
CBHW011238120626
46549CB00009B/3317